ADVENTUROUS
MODEL RAILWAY PLANS

CPLANS   30/6/03

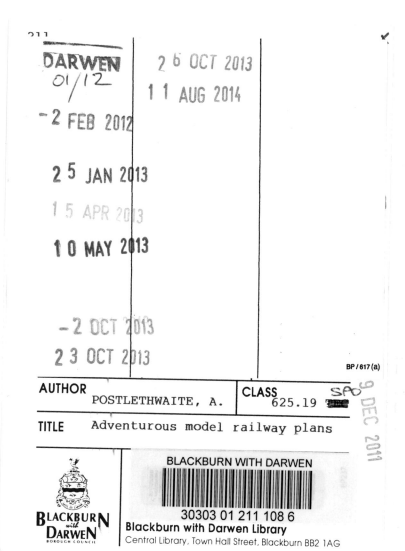

ADVENTUROUS
MODEL RAILWAY PLANS

ALAN POSTLETHWAITE

Patrick Stephens Limited
AN IMPRINT OF HAYNES PUBLISHING

© Alan Postlethwaite 2003 7/03

First published in 2003

A catalogue record for this book is available from the British Library

ISBN 1 85260 613 4

Library of Congress catalog card no. 2002117294   012111086

Published by Patrick Stephens Limited
an imprint of Haynes Publishing, Sparkford,
Yeovil, Somerset, BA22 7JJ, UK

Tel: 01963 442030 Fax: 01963 440001
Int. tel: +44 1963 442030 Int. fax: +44 1963 440001
E-mail: sales@haynes-manuals.co.uk
Web site: www.haynes.co.uk

Haynes North America, Inc.,
861 Lawrence Drive, Newbury Park,
California 91320, USA

Publisher's note
Most of the layout plans herein would need to be adapted and tailored to fit particular spaces, tastes and budgets as appropriate, and while recognising the practicalities of construction, the author does not offer mechanical, electrical or scenic designs in any detail, nor does he touch upon locomotive and rolling stock construction. So, sit back and enjoy operating some adventurous model railways in your mind.

Printed and bound in England by J. H. Haynes & Co. Ltd, Sparkford

While every effort is taken to ensure the accuracy of the information given in this book, no liability can be accepted by the author or publishers for any loss, damage or injury caused by errors in, or omissions from, the information given.

Contents

Introduction

I have a lively imagination. An ability to design things in my head was developed while studying engineering at City University and then during my career with the Central Electricity Generating Board. I could even play chess in my mind, but it was a love of model railways which first stimulated this capability. From my earliest set of Hornby clockwork tin-plate, through the years of Hornby Dublo, Peco Wonderful Wagons, fine-scale EM gauge and finally into American N gauge and my childrens' Lego trains, I have enjoyed designing and improving layouts – first in my head, then on paper and now on computer.

I have been inspired throughout by other people's model railways – in homes, clubrooms, exhibitions and magazines. I was nine or ten years old when introduced to Trix Twin, Rovex and pre-war Hornby electric O gauge sets which belonged to friends (or their fathers). On a Cubs' outing to the Boys Own Exhibition at the Royal Horticultural Halls in London, I discovered the British Railways O gauge exhibition layout - intended to recruit lads into careers with BR, but attracting me instead to countless model railway exhibitions ever since. I was 15 when I discovered *Model Railway News* after buying a batch of old magazines in my school library - the start of a collection of thousands. Many of my favourite

articles and books are listed in the References herein and are mentioned in the text as sources of inspiration.

A primary objective of good layouts is to captivate the viewers - to take them on journeys to some re-created landscape or town where their own imaginations can run wild – enjoying not only the trains but their setting and perhaps triggering some half-forgotten experience from childhood. Like a good painting, a model railway should be designed comprehensively rather than to depict the main subject in isolation. Indeed, the best layouts

are works of art which stir the soul.

A good way to get started in layout design is with a proprietary 'train set', using track and points in fixed-geometry pieces. These are available in gauges from Z to G. When such sets are laid out on the floor, table or lawn, the design can be readily modified until one achieves the desired operational objectives. The next step is to add buildings, signals and other accessories, especially people and road vehicles, so that the scene looks 'alive'. As the collection grows, one is eventually tempted to build a permanent layout, perhaps in the spare room,

Bob Alderman demonstrates soldering techniques at the 2001 NEC exhibition. He was one of a group of specialist modellers demonstrating different aspects of kit and scratch-building.

garage or attic. The final step is to replace fixed-geometry with more realistic variable-geometry track and to set it in realistic scenery. At that stage, a good imagination is essential, since a scenic layout is more difficult to modify once it has been built.

Standards of modelling vary from robust coarse-scale proprietary train sets (with steamroller wheels, deep flanges and fixed-radius curves), to delicate fine-scale kits, custom-built models and scratch-building in one's own workshop (with variable-radius curves and everything truly to scale). Scales and gauges have evolved over a century or so, with rationalisations to British, American and Continental standards. The most common found today are shown in the table below.

HO is the most popular American and Continental gauge and has no gauge error while OO is the most popular British gauge, and has the greatest gauge error. Some people can see this discrepancy, others cannot. The choice between the 4mm scales is essentially a declaration of modelling standard. EM and P4 are always fine-scale, covering not only track but everything from rolling stock to building detail. EM and P4 locomotives and rolling stock tend to be kit- or scratch-built. All the other gauges can be bought ready-to-run in standards ranging from 'coarse' to 'fine', which suits most modellers and all children.

There are many narrow gauge

Prior to the opening of the 2001 NEC exhibition, five stalwarts of the Wingfield Railway Group work on 'Durrant Road', their OO gauge modern-image layout which is based on their local station at Chesterfield. Four off-stage marshalling yards are shown here. Such yards are often used at exhibitions to provide a wide variety of trains attending the main station at the front of the layout.

derivatives of the scales below. Just two are featured in this book: Layout No. 27, *The Fustera Garden Line*; and, on page 98, a photograph of Malcolm Morgan's Gloucestershire garden line. Their respective scales and gauges are defined on page 96.

Seven basic layout configurations are illustrated overleaf. All model railways adhere to one or more of these, although often disguised by branches, extra loops, yards, tunnels, scenery and multiple levels of development. By using double-track, the layouts instantly become more complex with

interesting pointwork at the junctions. Developed from these configurations, 30 layout plans are presented herein. All are imaginary and have not been built except for my own *San Amji Railroad* (No. 8). The aim of these drawings is to inspire others to design and build large, interesting model railways which can stir the soul. A second objective is to take all readers on journeys of adventure around the various layouts – a form of escapism like a good painting, novel, television play or piece of music. One word of warning – do not build where the model is unwelcome! Remember that the alternative title of this book could be – *Thirty Good Ways to Ruin your Home!*

The locations for the layouts include domestic rooms, attics, garages, clubrooms, gardens, sheds and portable lines for exhibitions. Most are medium to

Name:	Z	N(UK)	N*	HO	OO	EM	P4	O	One
Scale (mm/ft)	1.4	2.06	1.9	3.5	4	4	4	7	10
Scale ratio 1:	220	148	160	87	76	76	76	43	32
Gauge (mm)	6.5	9	9	16.5	16.5	18.2	18.83	32	45
Standard gauge	4'3½"	4'4½"	4'8½"	4'8½"	4'1½"	4'6½"	4'8½"	4'5"	4'5"
Gauge error	-9%	-7%	0	0	-12%	-4%	0	-6%	-5%

* USA and the Continent

John Webb's EM gauge layout 'Ambergate' is prepared for service at the 2001 NEC exhibition. The mimic diagram of the control panel is clear, also the CCTV monitor for the hidden loops under the far hillside. Note also the cantilevers which support the lighting and the facia on the public viewing side, left.

high density, meaning that as much railway as possible is packed into a given space, enhanced by a little scenery. The exceptions are the garden lines which are low to medium density - just part of the garden landscape. Not included here are low-density indoor landscapes - such models make fine spectacles but require vast areas for basic railway operation. One of the best examples of landscape modelling is at the Pendon Museum near Abingdon. Here, their first-floor EM gauge railway wanders between vast fields of corn while hidden storage sidings nestle beneath whole villages of colourful fine-scale construction - the work of an army of dedicated landscape modellers over several decades.

To transform any of these plans into a successful model is a major task, which should not be underestimated. One needs space, money, time, craftsmanship, an appreciation of control principles and electrics, locomotives and rolling stock, a willingness to do maintenance and an ability to visualise the end product. Specific historical and geographic knowledge may also be required. Although magazines offer a wealth of practical advice on the construction of baseboards, control systems and other practicalities, the larger layouts are best tackled by clubs and groups so that the costs, skills, problems and chores can be shared between the members, with specialists emerging. Indeed, it is the sharing of model railways which gives the greatest satisfaction, throughout all the phases of design, construction, operation and exhibition.

Whilst recognising the practicalities of construction, I do not offer mechanical, electrical or scenic designs in any detail, nor do I touch upon locomotive and rolling stock construction. Two good practical reference books I can recommend are by Cyril Freezer (Ref. 1) and Norman Simmons (Ref. 2), while Roger Amos covers model railway electronics in Ref. 3. (See page 109 for these references.)

Most of the layout plans herein would need to be adapted and tailored to fit particular spaces, tastes and budgets as appropriate. So sit back and enjoy operating some adventurous plans. Remember that a model railway does not have to be an exact replica of the real thing. It a representation of a real railway, usually much shortened because of constraints of space, but with the capability of intensive services and a wide variety of train types. A good model railway is both a pleasure to operate and a joy to behold.

For ease of reference and efficient use of space, much of the narrative is in technical report style, with clear topic headings. Using the Draw facility of Microsoft Word, the diagrams make extensive use of colour to identify routes and/or electrical control sections. The primary aim here is to show the overall layout and operational routes clearly. Clutter is avoided by omitting minor accessories such as signals, signalboxes, footbridges, water cranes, roads and non-railway buildings. Finally, there is a wide choice in the method of control, the most common of which can be summarised as follows:

Clockwork manual control is used mainly in the larger scales.

Battery manual control (on-board, rechargeable) is used mainly for garden railways.

Live steam manual control (coal, gas or oil) is used mainly for Gauge One and larger.

FM radio can be used to control the regulator and reversing lever of live steam.

Digital control can be used for electrical control of all locomotives and auxiliaries using a single pair of wires from a central processor through one or more control units.

Section control is the traditional electrical method, using one controller per section of track.

Cab control is a variation of section control but with double-pole section switches added so that a train's journey can be controlled smoothly from a single cab, illustrated as follows:

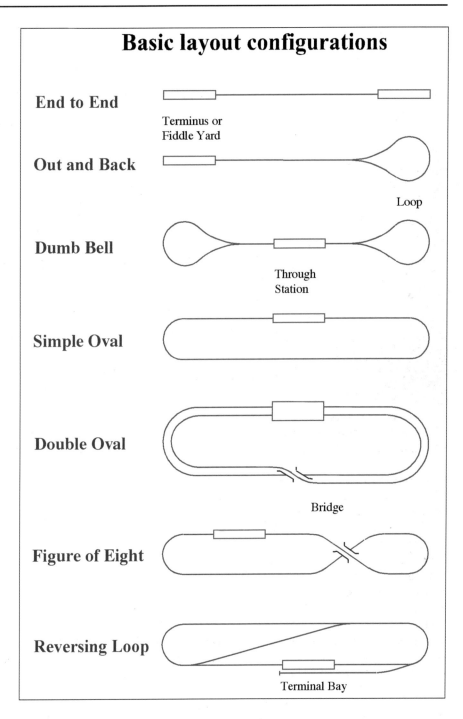

Basic layout configurations

End to End — Terminus or Fiddle Yard

Out and Back — Loop

Dumb Bell — Through Station

Simple Oval

Double Oval — Bridge

Figure of Eight

Reversing Loop — Terminal Bay

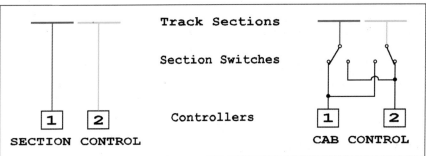

Track Sections

Section Switches

Controllers

SECTION CONTROL   CAB CONTROL

1 2   1 2

1

The Chiltern Link

Summary description: An OO gauge triple oval on two levels with stations and yards from the Big Four railways of the 1923 Grouping - GWR, LMS, LNER and SR. It represents an imaginary cross-country joint line between, say, Wokingham and Aylesbury (with some Metropolitan stock thrown in).

Inspiration: Visits to my wife's grandparents' flat in Bexhill-on-Sea where I designed a layout in my mind for their first-floor sitting room while enjoying afternoon tea and scones. Ref. 4 shows a similar lounge layout built in O gauge on two levels.

Design features:
- An OO gauge layout to fit a large Victorian lounge measuring 4.1m by 2.8m overall.
- Two high-level termini to fit into the recesses to either side of the bay window.
- A double-track oval on the lower level with a through-station.
- Additional loops at both levels to create a triple oval.
- A goods depot on the lowest level along the wall below the door.
- No turntable (requiring balanced operation for tender locomotives).

Control principles: Cab control and wandering leads for four drivers. Point operation and section switching are from a mimic control panel at the front of the layout just above eye level, an idea taken from Ref. 5.

Operation: With so many ovals, continuous operation is possible with just occasional visits to the terminal platforms – particularly suitable for using tank engines only. For more authentic operation (with the inclusion of tender engines), a balanced timetable can be used in end-to-end mode as follows:
- Anticlockwise, all passenger trains terminate at the SR station.
- Clockwise, alternate passenger trains terminate at the GWR and LNER stations.
- Goods trains run between the GWR and LMS yards, calling at the LNER yard.
- Motor trains run between the LMS and SR bay, reversing in the LNER station or in the hidden loops.

Balance is achieved by transferring locos between SR and GWR and between LMS and LNER. For example, Loco 1 heads a passenger train from SR to LNER then runs forward and reverses via **B** to LMS. Loco 2 then runs from **C** via **F** into LNER to head the passenger train back to SR. Loco 1 then heads a goods train from LMS to GWR. This releases Loco 3 which runs via **B** into **C** to await duty on the next passenger train to arrive in LNER.

Construction: Baseboards are Sundeala board on timber supports and wall brackets. Straight sections of the upper stations have piano hinges for access to the tunnels. The switch panel spans the front just above eye level (angled forwards) with the main layout lighting above, to create a stunning panorama as one enters the room, like looking out of an aircraft cockpit.

Accessories: Signalboxes, footbridges, subways, platform canopies and possibly an overall roof for the SR station; townscape murals behind the perimeter stations and at the buffer stop ends.

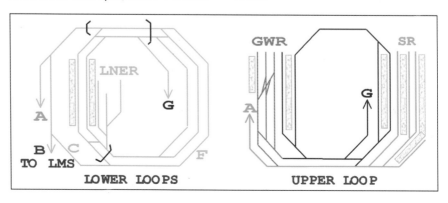

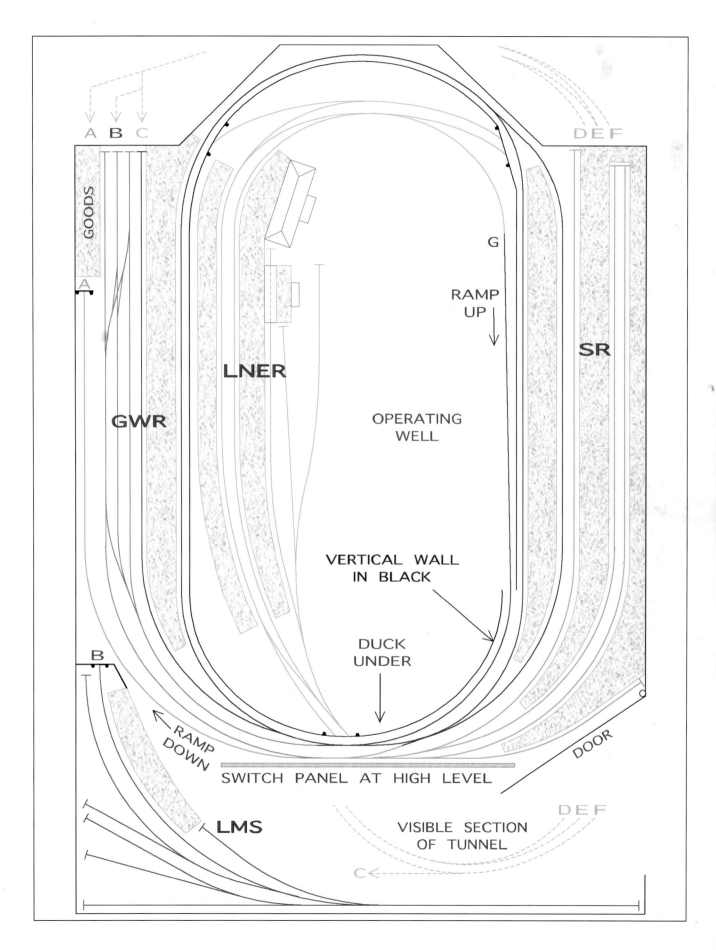

A B C

DEF

GOODS

A

G

RAMP
UP

SR

LNER

GWR

OPERATING
WELL

VERTICAL WALL
IN BLACK

DUCK
UNDER

B

RAMP
DOWN

DOOR

SWITCH PANEL AT HIGH LEVEL

LMS

DEF

VISIBLE SECTION
OF TUNNEL

C

2

The Highland Garden Railway

Summary description: A figure-of-eight indoor section and an out-and-back garden section, operated together or independently according to the weather, mood and the number of operators.

Inspiration: The indoor section was inspired by the dining room of some lodgings from my student days - a long L-shaped Edwardian room, crying out for a double-track around the walls and a long terminus down the middle.

Leisurely operation was envisaged – a style inspired by John Langan's EM gauge layout *Presson* (Ref. 6). The Highland setting derived from our honeymoon and later holidays, with train journeys made in sleet and snow from Inverness to Kyle of Lochalsh and Thurso. The layout of Inverness, however, is modelled on Stamford, not the real Inverness (see photographs on pages 16 and 17).

Indoor design features:
- A double-track main line with three reversing loops.
- A showpiece peninsular terminus with a goods yard.
- Plenty of space for viewing and operating.
- A discrete MPD with turntable.
- A branch terminus with a goods yard or quarry.
- Two hidden storage sidings under the terminus.

Control principles: If funds allow, digital control is ideal for operating all locomotives and points. A good

alternative is cab control, with up to six controllers in use for the indoor section, namely: Up Main, Down Main, Terminus, Goods Yard, MPD, and Branch.

An indoor signalman then controls all main line points and section switches from a seated position in the bottom well, using voice or headphone communication. Points and uncouplers within the stations and yards are operated manually by the four local drivers.

Cab control of the garden section uses wandering leads in the alley and sunken path, connected to a weather-protected switching panel in the bottom section of the French windows. As with all model railways, personal safety is paramount – always adhere to manufacturers' instructions and take advice from qualified technicians when in doubt.

Operation:
- For the indoor section alone, there is normally one train on each main line (red and blue), operating in either figure-of-eight mode or as a dumb bell (using the gold and pink reversing loops).
- Blue can also be operated as a simple oval using the green-pink outer loop.
- The terminus uses roads 1, centre and 2 respectively for passenger arrivals, servicing and departures.
- Branch and goods arrivals use roads 3 and 4, having an engine run-round facility.
- To turn, tender locos must

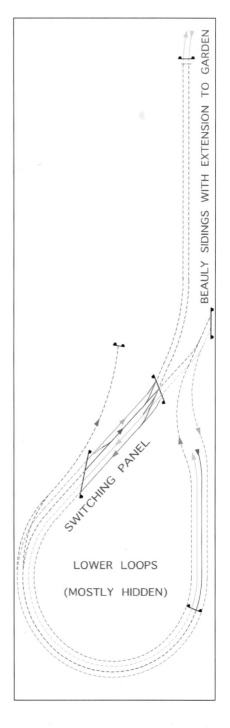

BEAULY SIDINGS WITH EXTENSION TO GARDEN

SWITCHING PANEL

LOWER LOOPS

(MOSTLY HIDDEN)

cross the main line (twice) to the MPD – made easier when in dumb bell or oval mode since only the down main (red) is then in use at this junction.

- On dry winter days, services can be extended out and back to Dingwall, controlled by looking out of the French windows.

Construction: The indoor main line is supported on wall brackets, with a propped bridge across the French windows at the top end. These doors are permanently shut; indeed, the bottom half can be bricked up, with new windows above together with a ventilation fan. For Inverness terminus, the lower loops and branch line, Sundeala baseboards are laid on a combination of wall and floor supports, with lift-out sections at both stations for access to the six hidden points.

The main platforms at Inverness, Dingwall and Ullapool are sized for six-coach steam trains in EM gauge, giving overall dimensions of 6.2m by 2.3m for the dining room and 7.0m by 4.6m for the garden (excluding the alley where Ullapool measures 5.4m by 0.5m). For gardens, O gauge is more usual and more effective than EM, requiring all the above dimensions to be increased by 175 per cent. To fit my old lodgings in O gauge, the basic configuration can remain but with shorter trains and some simplification of the stations. The indoor section might take a group some three to five years to complete. Construction of the outdoor section would also take three to five years, phased either in series or in parallel.

Indoor accessories:
Drumnadrochit is fully modelled with fine-scale buildings, an approach road and motor vehicles. At Inverness, buildings are left mostly to the imagination, with the emphasis upon railway movements. Ceiling spot lights would bring out the best features.

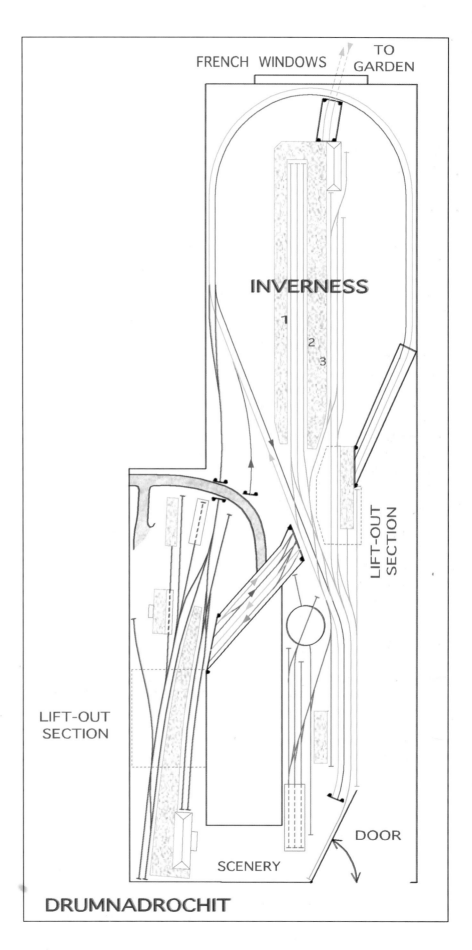

Historical setting: In a reversal of true history - following the Jacobite victory at Culloden, Highland culture, commerce and industry prospered and grew. It was centred upon the twin cities of Dingwall and Inverness, together with the deep-water Atlantic port of Ullapool. Railways flourished accordingly, with some convoluted loops and cut-offs around Dingwall. In such a scenario, the map below shows how the Highland Railway might have developed in the region. Note the three routes to Ullapool.

Garden extension of the Highland Railway:

Inspiration: Articles in *Railway Modeller* on two fine O gauge garden railways: David Jenkinson's *Kendal Branch* (Ref. 7) and Ken Payne's *A New Beginning* (Ref. 8). They took me back to my student lodgings which had a large back garden and a long side alley, and I resolved to extend Beauly sidings through the French windows into a whole new world of 'the great outdoors'. Dingwall station and quay were inspired by P. D. Hancock's *Craig & Mertonford Light Railway* (Ref. 9) while Ullapool quay was inspired by Kyle of Lochalsh (see photograph on page 16) and by Port Dicksby on Jeff Colledge's extensive *North Midland Railway* (Ref. 10).

Design features: My first attempt was a single-track spiral leading down to a double-track oval with a low-level through-station and a narrow terminus in the alley. This was visually and operationally uninteresting. Instead, I wanted a layout with multiple modes of operation, and this led to the 'hourglass' design, creating some intriguing routes and a sense of long-distance travel. Visual breaks are provided by the viaduct and the city development at Dingwall. Steps from the sunken path lead to the lawns and segregate the Dingwall complex from the long line to Ullapool. Built in the alley, Ullapool is necessarily long and narrow, with the MPD located at the far end (by the dustbins).

Operation: The garden section can be run by two or three operators, with services from Ullapool - out and back to Dingwall - and end to end to Conon Bridge. With additional operators available, services can be extended to the indoor section. Full timetable operation to all stations would need about seven operators.

Construction: The viaduct is reinforced concrete, cast in situ, with a wooden truss bridge to the French windows. The elevated main line around the periphery is laid upon a stone causeway, with mountain scenery painted on the

fences. The lawns and garden seat are important, creating restful places to contemplate and observe.

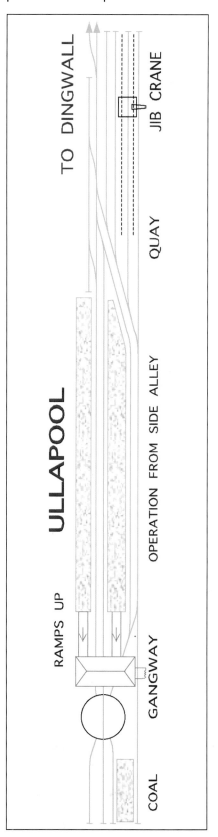

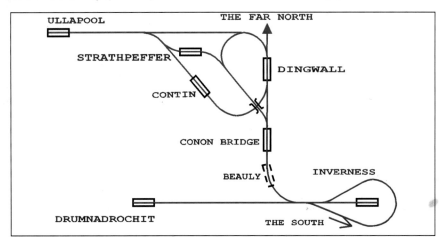

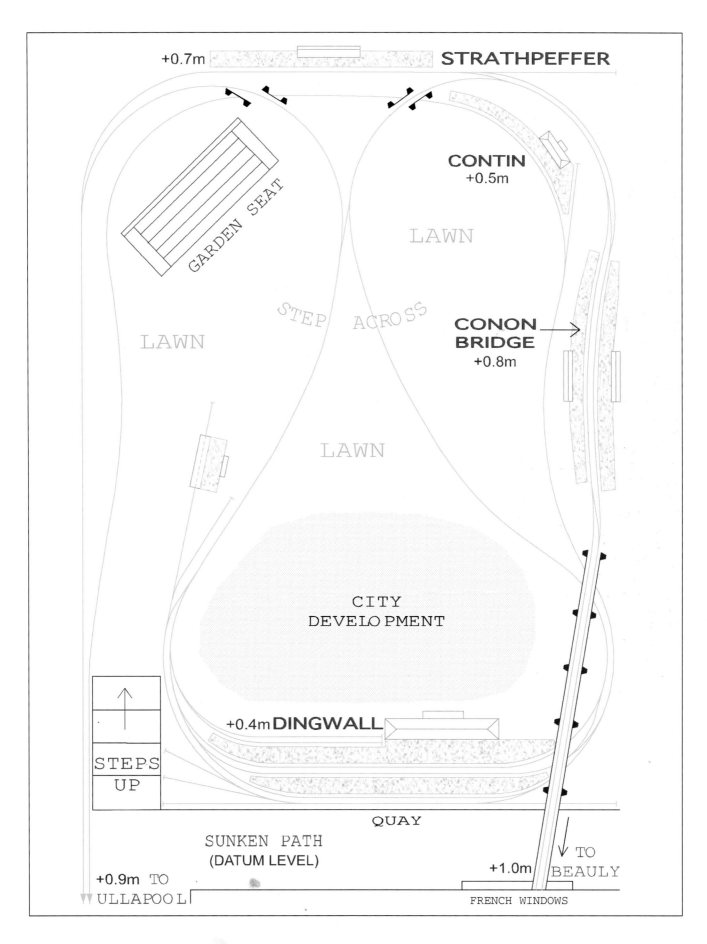

STRATHPEFFER +0.7m

CONTIN +0.5m

GARDEN SEAT

LAWN

STEP ACROSS

LAWN

CONON BRIDGE +0.8m

LAWN

CITY DEVELOPMENT

+0.4m **DINGWALL**

STEPS UP

QUAY

SUNKEN PATH (DATUM LEVEL)

+0.9m TO ULLAPOOL

+1.0m TO BEAULY

FRENCH WINDOWS

Stamford Town inspired the indoor terminus and junction of Layout No. 2. This modest Great Northern terminus had a goods yard (centre) and a train shed with an island platform (right) plus two sidings. The Midland connecting spur came in from the left, seen here with a Fowler 0-6-0 making heavy exhaust with a mineral train.

Kyle of Lochalsh inspired the outdoor terminus of Layout No. 2, seen here in 1957 with a busy quay and train to Dingwall headed by LMS 4-6-0 Class 5MT No. 45179. All the stations on this line have an air of bleakness, freshness and informality. The mountains of Skye make an awesome backdrop. (Hugh Ballantyne)

The real Inverness inspired the Swansea terminus of Layout No. 7 – a station of two halves. These ultra-wide platforms serve trains to Kyle of Lochalsh and the Far North, while Perth and Aberdeen trains use separate platforms and sheds on the far side. Photographed in 1967 (post steam, pre-DMU).

Maldon East in half relief is a possible prototype for the GER terminus of Layout No. 3. Built in Jacobean style and with a great canopy, it is a major project if modelled in fine-scale. Photographed in 1963, with a DMU.

3

A Great Eastern Loft Layout

Summary description: A simple oval around my old loft, with one through-station and a terminus, suitable for P4 standards of precision modelling.

Inspiration: While fitting a new water tank in my loft in Kent, I noticed that there was just space through the trusses for a 4mm double-track line to be laid around the periphery. There was also space for a terminus between two trusses in the central area. As the entire layout would necessarily be level, the flatness of East Anglia sprang to mind, as did some of P. M. Alexander's evocative East Anglian railway photographs. Regarding the station layout, I was influenced by several model railways set in Suffolk, especially those of Iain Rice with his fine-scale buildings and a water mill (Refs. 11 and 12). The result is a Great Eastern secondary line to nowhere.

Design features:
- An outer oval for passenger and mixed trains.

- An inner oval for freight and mixed trains.
- A simple terminus with a turntable, sidings and a station building (see photo on page 17).
- A quality through-station with goods sidings, a wharf and a mill (see photos on page 20).

Control principles:
- Three electrical sections – Outer, Inner and Terminus – with cab control switches.
- Normally two-person operation – one at the terminus and one at the through-station.
- The outer loop can be put on auto, with trains calling at the through-station in alternate directions.
- Predominantly manual operation of points, screw- and three-link couplings.

Operation: Passenger trains start clockwise from the terminus, presently reversing in the through-station, using a fresh tender engine from the MPD.
Short passenger and mixed

passenger-freight trains operate on a similar sequence but with tank engines running round at the through-station. The bay (top right) stores coaches and auto-trains. Freight trains run mainly on the inner oval, with some leisurely spells of shunting.

Types of roof:
A. Purlins run the length of the roof, supported on posts. They are often found in bungalows, giving a clear working area but with limited head clearance at the sides. Layouts Nos 14, 26 and 28 are laid out entirely within the purlins. See also the photograph on page 99.
B. Prefabricated trusses are more common on houses with a steeper roof pitch. They give a more obstructed working area but with a greater head clearance.

Construction: The layout measures 4.3m by 4.0m. A loft conversion can be a major expenditure which needs to be done professionally (Ref. 13). It is generally cheaper than moving to

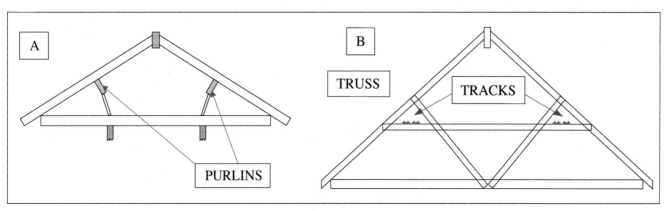

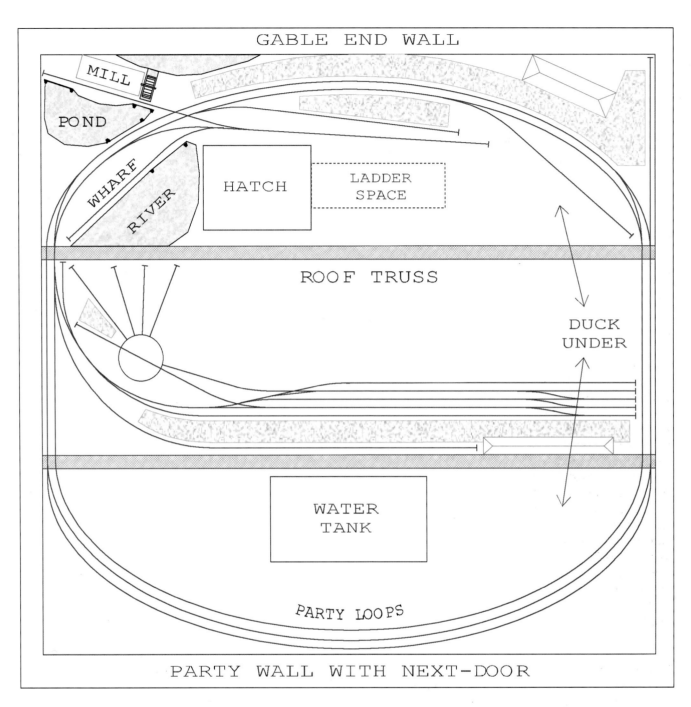

GABLE END WALL

MILL

POND

WHARF

RIVER

HATCH

LADDER SPACE

ROOF TRUSS

DUCK UNDER

WATER TANK

PARTY LOOPS

PARTY WALL WITH NEXT-DOOR

a larger house. Such a conversion includes floor-boarding, insulated wall-boards and sloping ceiling-boards, lighting, a power supply, heating and ventilating provisions, smoke alarms and fire extinguishers. To prevent distortions of the railway baseboards, allowance must be made for free sliding movement as roof timbers expand thermally according to season.

For my old house in Kent,

access was via the hatch, requiring a folding aluminium ladder and a hatch cover (for walking on when the ladder is down). A window is an optional extra – set in the gable wall - facing north. The level baseboard rests upon the roof trusses, wall brackets at the two ends and upon floor posts elsewhere. Once converted, the loft becomes a railway paradise, with no interference from other household activities.

Accessories: All buildings, bridges and yard accessories are built to a high standard of realism, together with scenic backdrops in semi-relief at both stations.

Full semaphore signalling is controlled electrically with 'double-bounce' of the arms. With signal bells to complete the setting, this is a railway to stand back and admire, not one of intensive train services.

Some inspirational buildings on the Maldon branch for the GER through-station of Layout No. 3. Wickham Bishops is a fine example of Cottage Orné with a steeply pitched roof, tall, ornate chimneys and cosmetic timbering. The scene brings out the flatness of the Essex countryside, interspersed with trees and a mill chimney.

This great brick mill and lock on the River Nene at Thrapston, Northamptonshire, was also inspirational for Layout No. 3. Rivers and canals can look splendid when blended with model railways. Some fine examples are Peter Denny's 'Buckingham Great Central' (Ref. 23) and Andy Jones's 'Canalside' (see photograph on page 53). The Nene is better known by enthusiasts for the Nene Valley Railway, preserved for steam and diesel.

These 1962 scenes from Farringdon helped to inspire Layout No. 4. Above: Looking east are the tunnels leading to Moorgate. The Metropolitan Line is on the left together with three EMU sidings in the centre. Smithfield Market looms above the twin tunnels of the Widened Lines where a DMU is destined for Welwyn Garden City.

Below: Looking west, with Farringdon Goods Yard on the left, the Widened Lines start a steep descent to cross under the Metropolitan Line. A single crossover with slip points connects the two systems. Note the cable arch.

4

Metrocity Exhibition Layout

Summary description: A permanent exhibition layout on five levels, with interchange stations between four semi-independent systems – the Metropolitan Line – the GWR/GCR main line – the Widened Lines – and the Bakerloo tube line. See the overall layout plan overleaf.

Inspiration: Many business trips on the world's first underground railway, between Paddington and the City, invoking a sense of history and revealing the many terminal platforms and interchanges. I was also inspired by steam + underground model railways, notably the Model Railway Club's N gauge exhibition layout, *Copenhagen Fields* (Ref. 14). Also, *Grove Park* (Ref. 15), *Epton* (Ref. 16), the Gauge One Association (Ref. 17), C. A. Parfitt's under-the-floorboards system (Ref. 18) and R. D. Hart's Underground review (Ref. 19).

The Metropolitan Line:
A great convoluted dumb bell with EMUs operating end to end from Liverpool Street (tunnel siding) to Baker Street (clockwise) and to Edgware Road (anticlockwise). In addition, an electric locomotive-

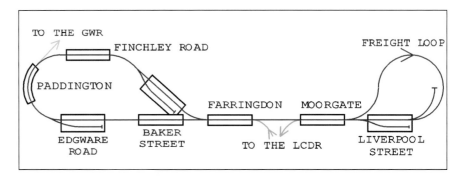

hauled passenger train operates out and back from the bay at Liverpool Street, with a second locomotive stored there.

There are freight connections with the GWR at Paddington and with the LCDR at Farringdon. Northbound freight trains run directly from the LCDR into Farringdon, whereas southbound freight trains take the Liverpool Street loop first.

The GWR/GCR main line:
End-to-end operation between Paddington and Marylebone, running parallel to the Metropolitan and Bakerloo lines at Finchley Road. Passenger trains are representative of post-war express and local steam stock, plus some first-generation DMUs. Each terminus has a turntable, with principal locomotive storage at

Paddington. One half of Marylebone handles general goods, while Paddington has just a long parcels platform (an extension of Platform 1). Operators at Paddington and Marylebone are concerned mainly with shunting and locomotive movements. Freight trains connect with the Metropolitan Line at Paddington. Built on the uppermost level, Paddington and its approach dominates the entire layout.

The Widened Lines:
Historically, the 'Widened Lines' was built by the Metropolitan Railway but was worked mainly by the GNR, Midland and LCDR. It runs from St Pancras and King's Cross to Moorgate, with a triangular spur to the LCDR. It became a principal north-south freight transfer route as well as a

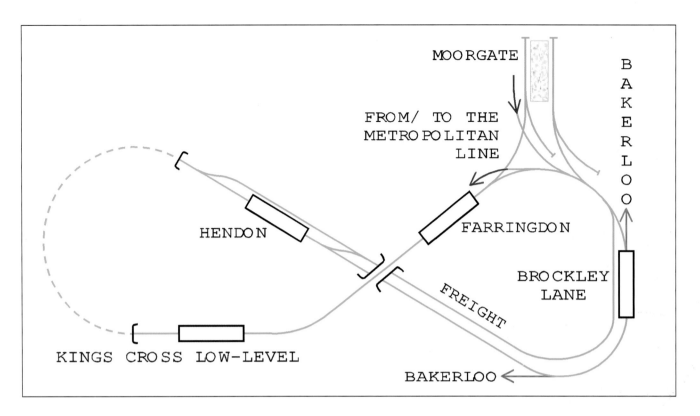

commuting route to the City.

Built as a giant figure-of-eight, the model configuration is disguised by other railways which pass over it. It represents the steam era from the 1920s to the 1960s, including pre-Grouping rolling stock and condensing tank engines. Using the two terminal platforms and loco spurs at Moorgate, passenger trains reverse occasionally to work in end-to-end mode. Freight trains transfer to the Metropolitan Line at Farringdon, often running through to Marylebone. There are suburban goods yards at both Brockley Lane (LCDR) and Hendon (Midland Railway).

The Bakerloo Line:
A simple oval with automatic operation, using a mix of 1938 stock from the Bakerloo/Northern lines and 1927 stock from the Piccadilly/Central lines. The two surface stations are shared with the LCDR, Met. and GCR. Edgware Road is modelled clockwise only, King's Cross is the former narrow island platform of the Northern Line and Baker Street has split levels.

In a break from true history, the LCDR suburban station at Brockley Lane is shared with the Bakerloo Line – part of an imaginary extension from Elephant & Castle through Camberwell and Peckham to Greenwich Park. There were many true examples in North London of shared lines.

Construction: Phased over some ten years or more, construction would start at Level 0 and work up to Level 8. Crossings require a minimum difference of two levels (eg L6 – L4). This permanent layout requires a large hall, basement or mezzanine. Sized for seven-coach main line trains and five-car Underground EMUs, the layout measures 7.2m x 3.6m in 4mm scale. A clearance of 1 to 2 metres must then be added on all sides for access, control and viewing.

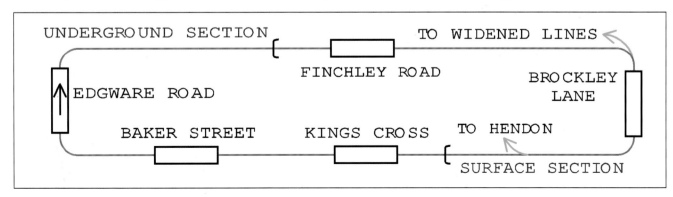

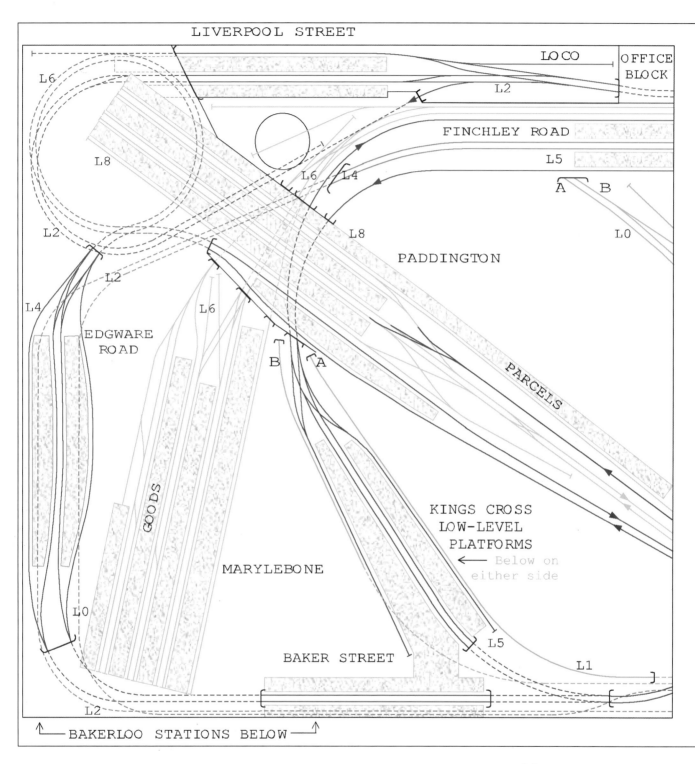

LIVERPOOL STREET

LOCO

OFFICE BLOCK

L6

L2

L8

FINCHLEY ROAD

L5

A   B

L2

L2

L6   L4

L0

L8

PADDINGTON

L4

EDGWARE ROAD

L6

PARCELS

B   A

GOODS

KINGS CROSS LOW-LEVEL PLATFORMS

← Below on either side

L0

MARYLEBONE

L5

BAKER STREET

L1

L2

↑— BAKERLOO STATIONS BELOW —↑

Control principles: A specialist Control Group would consider options and make recommendations. The basic choice is between one comprehensive central control consol and a multiplicity of local panels spread around the periphery and in the wells. The decision would depend upon the character of the club and the number of operators in prospect. With an army of reliable club members, local control would be most enjoyable, making intensive use of the yards. At the other extreme, with a small number of professional operators, central control would be essential, having many automatic features but making infrequent use of the yards. Such an exhibition layout would make a wonderful extension to London's Transport Museum at Covent Garden; the main deterrent is the cost of the premises.

24

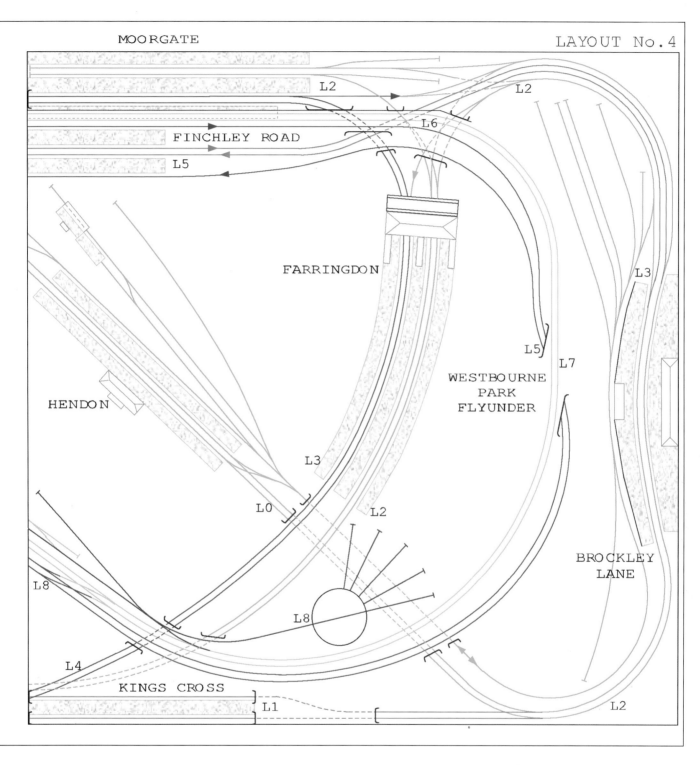

MOORGATE

L2

L2

FINCHLEY ROAD

L6

L5

L2

FARRINGDON

L3

L5

L7

WESTBOURNE
PARK
FLYUNDER

HENDON

L3

L0

L2

BROCKLEY
LANE

L8

L8

L4

KINGS CROSS

L1

L2

Signalling: A specialist Signalling Group would design and install a mix of semaphores and colour-lights. Whilst lineside signals might be operated from local control panels to communicate with adjacent operators, it is simpler to use automatic operation, triggered by approaching trains and point positions.

Accessories: The ends of Paddington, Marylebone and Farringdon are finished with a concourse and part-building, also an overall roof - but not too long otherwise trains become lost. There is scope for much urban building, particularly around Edgware Road, Marylebone and Brockley Lane (always leaving provision for maintenance access to the trackwork). Alternatively, additional goods and train sidings could be incorporated at Farringdon, Baker Street, Paddington and Edgware Road.

5

The Crantock Railway

Summary description: A coarse-scale reversing loop with low-level ovals, also a through-station and a high-level terminus, offering intensive services with a great variety of train types and locomotive movements.

Inspiration: A permanent Hornby Dublo garage layout, built for my childhood friend David by his father (see diagram below). The single-track oval rose on the near side to cross a short branch to a terminal platform and a goods siding. It was beautifully finished with roads, fields, houses, animals and people. Point (**e**), uncoupler (**u**) and signal (**s**) were electrically operated. The operational restrictions are clear, especially if I tell you that the principal locomotive was Pacific *Sir Nigel Gresley* – looking resplendent in LNER blue but a little out of place in the short platform or in the goods shed. Realism was improved by the addition of an 0-6-2 tank but the inability remained to run round, reverse or store trains. Decades later, inspired by born-again Hornby Dublo

layouts in magazines and at exhibitions, I redeveloped the Crantock Railway as described opposite.

Design features: Track geometry and accessories are suitable for 3-rail Hornby Dublo or modern equivalent. A single-track branch

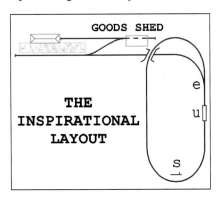

THE INSPIRATIONAL LAYOUT

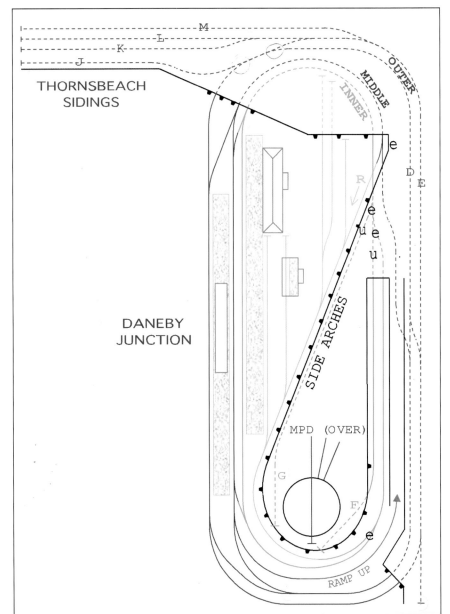

rises above the main line to create a tunnel on the latter. The high-level terminus has goods and carriage sidings, also an MPD with turntable. The main line is a three-track oval with a through-station and whole-train storage sidings. The reversing loop **R** is integral with a low-level goods yard. Bays at both stations serve push-pull/EMU/DMU trains.

Control principles:
- Six section controllers: Top Station, Top Yard, Outer, Middle, Inner, Bottom Yard.
- The MPD to have a three-position supply switch: Top Station, Off, and Top Yard.
- Electrical operation of four points (**e**) and two uncouplers (**u**); all others manual.
- Siding isolation mainly by point position, plus some push-buttons for siding ends.

Operation: A passenger set from storage sidings **A** or **B** is marshalled in Crantock; a tender loco arrives from the MPD; the train then runs to Daneby; is held in hidden sidings **D** or **E**; continues through Daneby; across the reversing loop **R**, and reverses into siding **F**. The loco then transfers to a goods train in Daneby Yard.

A new loco later transfers from a fuel train in bottom siding **G** to head the passenger train back to Crantock and then to reverse it into sidings **A** or **B** before returning to the MPD and the turntable.

With a 2-6-4 tank engine on a long passenger set, alternative methods of low-level turn-round are possible using hidden sidings **D** or **E** - either by running round - or by running forward round the oval - or by using a spare loco from Thornsbeach storage sidings **J**, **K**, **L** and **M**.

Short push-pull/EMU/DMU trains rotate between Crantock bay, Daneby bay, Thornsbeach storage sidings and top storage siding **C**.

General goods trains run between Crantock Yard and Daneby Yard, using loco transfers with trains held in sidings **F** and **G**. Two fuel trains (respectively coal and oil) run between top siding **H** and bottom siding **G**, departing simultaneously and using low-level locomotive transfers with goods and passenger trains. Note that storage sidings **F** and **G** are visible through the arches.

Construction: Intended as a permanent layout with all-round access and viewing, using Sundeala board on timber supports, with built-in controllers and switches. Although more difficult, it could be built as a portable layout with eight baseboards, bolted together. It measures 3.0m by 2.2m overall in OO gauge.

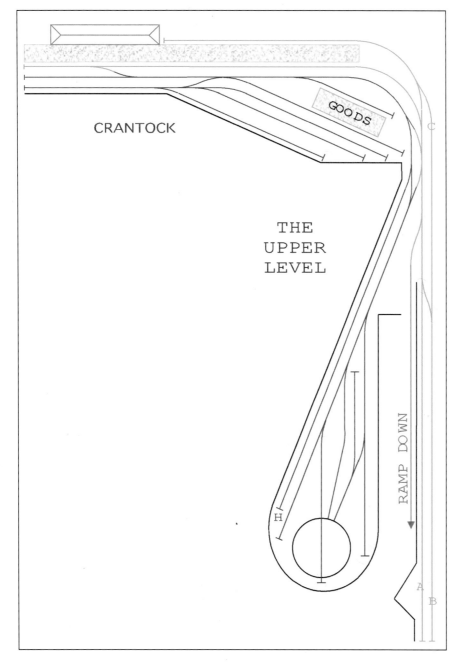

6

An Independent Lounge Railway

Summary description: A 4mm end-to-end railway which spirals two and a half times around a through-lounge, with a showpiece top station down the centre.

Inspiration: When Marion and I were first married, we lived for six years in a modern house on the North Downs by the LCDR main line. Having no television, many evenings were spent around the coal fire - toasting crumpets, listening to the radio and kit-bashing. Marion concentrated on Jacobean embroidery while I preferred EM gauge rolling stock.

Our products were lined up occasionally on the mantelpiece and this set my mind racing - to extend the track around the walls and up the middle of the lounge (evicting us in the process). The idea was to provide a great display ground for my models - mostly Southern at that time, with a touch of GWR, LMS and BR (see photograph on page 65). The railway is independent, however, having no physical connection with other lines.

The result was a long, single-track main line with a turntable at either end. It could be set anywhere remote in the British Isles, but the peninsular terminus with the (red) loop below was inspired by Bronar on C. L. Fry's *Irish International System* (Ref. 20) – his original 7mm complex layout at Churchtown which included an extensive tramway and a narrow gauge system. The fine new layout at Malahide Castle (near Dublin) also bears C. L. Fry's name but is much simpler in configuration, comprising mainly concentric ovals in a huge purpose-built hall.

Design features:
- A single-track spiral around four walls of a lounge, with a central peninsular.
- Easy access, with a lifting bridge across the door.
- A sliding main door and patio doors (for access to the tunnels).
- A goods yard at each of three stations, plus industrial sidings.
- A turntable at either end with principal locomotive storage at the MPD on the top level.

Control principles:
- Four cab controllers with wandering leads.
- Manual operation of points and couplings.

Operation: With two or three operators available, timetable operation can be used, with simultaneous departure of two trains from the termini. Single-person operation is also possible, with plenty of time to admire the leisurely progress of one's favourite train.

Construction: The peninsular baseboard has wooden supports with storage shelves below. Wall brackets are used extensively for the peripheral line, together with one curved viaduct, one arched bridge and one lifting truss bridge (for people access). The right-hand wall has two levels of railway development with a 0.3m difference of level. Designed for seven-coach trains in 4mm scale, the room measures 5.0m x 2.5m overall. On reflection, I have to admit that the fairly tight curves are more suitable for coarse-scale OO gauge than EM. The trackwork could be up and running within a few years, but the scenic work and accessories might take five years or more to approach perfection.

Accessories: Scenic development around the periphery, with plastic rocks, hilly murals and foam trees. There are no roads or non-railway buildings but the many goods yards, loco yards and industrial sidings cry out for a colourful population of people, road vehicles, cranes, staithes, storage tanks, huts and other accessories. Such a showpiece layout also demands full semaphore signalling - probably a mix of electric and wire-in-tube operation. As in Dublin, miniature lighting in the stations and trains would be accompanied by automatic sequencing to dim and reactivate the room lighting (mainly spots).

Postscript: In the event, we preferred to live with the coal fire and crumpets, but I still enjoy the model railway in my mind. Layout No. 16 is a more realistic (portable) proposition for my EM gauge models.

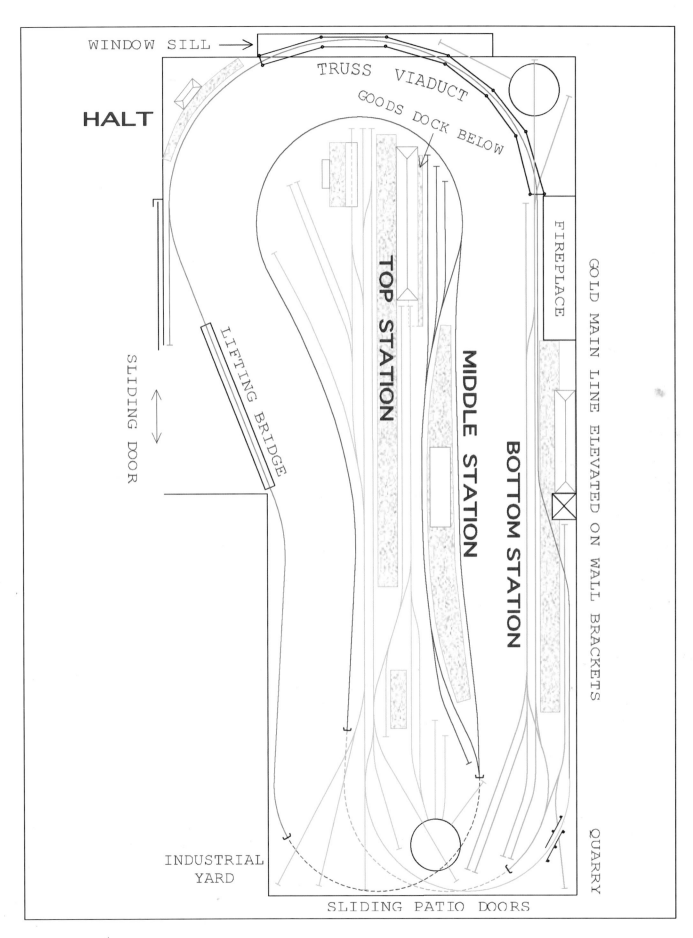

WINDOW SILL →

HALT

TRUSS VIADUCT

GOODS DOCK BELOW

FIREPLACE

GOLD MAIN LINE ELEVATED ON WALL BRACKETS

SLIDING DOOR

LIFTING BRIDGE

TOP STATION

MIDDLE STATION

BOTTOM STATION

INDUSTRIAL YARD

SLIDING PATIO DOORS

QUARRY

7

The Swansea Vale Garden Line

Summary description: An O gauge reversing loop set in my former Kentish garden with an outdoor terminus and an indoor through-station.

Inspiration: It is a natural extension of the ideas of Railway No. 6, but with only one wall of our through-lounge occupied by the railway. The two-directional terminus was inspired by Inverness (see photograph on page 17) but became Swansea St Thomas after reading a short article by Mike Christensen in *Model Railway Journal* No. 49.

Design features:
- A long main line oval - single-track with a passing station.
- A showpiece viaduct for the reversing loop, passing over the end of the outdoor terminus.
- A triangular junction to the terminus, requiring no turntable for tender locomotives.
- A goods yard and bay platforms at either station.

Control principles: Cab control with five electrical sections. Full operation requires two people - one outside for the terminus - the other indoors by the patio door for everything else.

Operation: Seven-coach express trains to Birmingham, Derby and Manchester depart twice daily from Platform 2, returning via the (red) reversing loop. Shorter stopping trains to Brecon and Hereford operate from Platform 3, using the triangular junction to run out and back in either direction. Local push-pull trains rotate between Platforms 1 and 4 and Colbren.

Long goods trains run from Swansea Yard to Birmingham, returning via the reversing loop. Local goods trains call at Colbren Yard. The overall effect is of long spectacular runs, balanced by interesting movements in the Swansea complex.

Construction: The property slopes gently upwards from front to back, measuring 25m by 12m. In the front garden, the line is laid on a concrete viaduct, with a removable bridge across the path to the front door. In the back

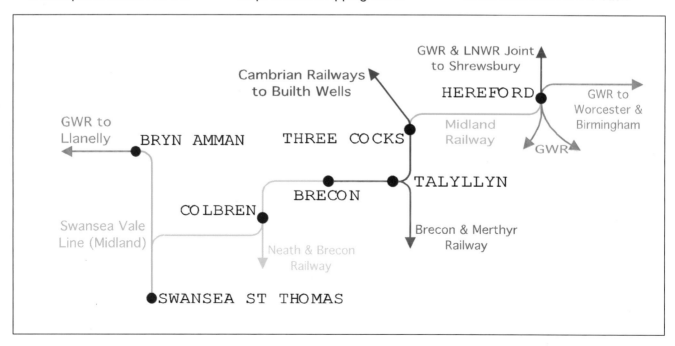

garden, the main line is laid on a stone causeway. The terminus is located at the lowest level with stepping stones across the triangular junction to the back garden. The back and side garden is landscaped to represent South Wales. Indoors, the baseboard is laid on storage cupboards with scenic backdrops.

Historical setting: The Midland Railway reached Swansea in 1874 via the GWR to Hereford, its own line to Three Cocks, then the Cambrian, the Brecon & Merthyr and the Neath & Brecon railways and finally over the Swansea Vale line which the Midland had absorbed in 1855. As well as giving the Midland its own access to Swansea docks, a stated benefit of this new connection was to provide fast delivery of goods made in Swansea to the Midlands, the North of England and via Hull to the Baltic Sea and Russia. All that remains today is a two-mile stretch of the Swansea Vale line which is preserved for steam and diesel operation on the outskirts of Swansea.

The real Swansea St Thomas had two platforms of unequal lengths, with a goods connection to the East Dock. The triangular junction is invented, allowing local Great Western trains to enter St Thomas.

With the through-station based upon the Neath & Brecon Railway, the result is a colourful mix of trains and services. The era depicted could be pre-Grouping, LMS or early BR.

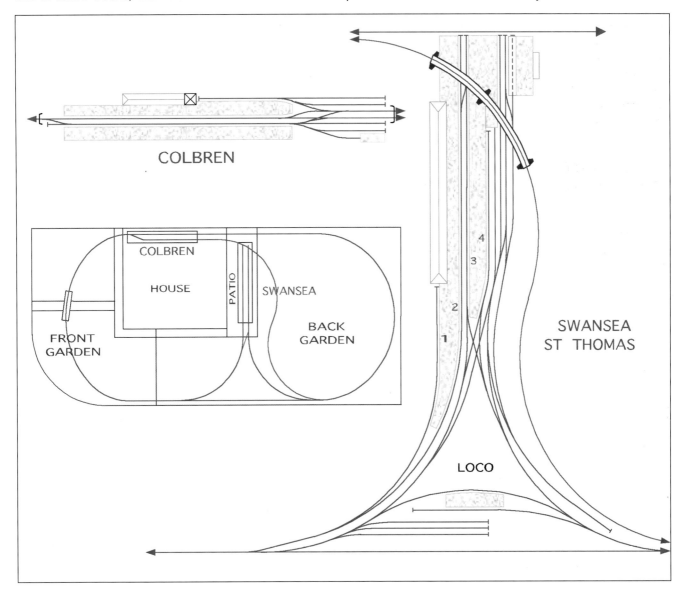

8

The San Amji Garage Railroad

Summary description: A scenic out-and-back American N gauge real layout in coarse-scale on three levels.

Inspiration: Following our house move to Gloucestershire, I continued to build EM gauge models for some years. I even started a long baseboard in the hall, bracketed to one wall. But with both our children at primary school, family needs always came first. Then we inherited a piano which took pride of place in the hall, evicting the embryonic model railway. So my thoughts turned to something completely different - American N gauge using ready-to-run trains on a baseboard spanning the width of our garage (with the car bonnet underneath). It is named after my family's initials - Alan, Marion, Jane and Ian.

Regarding layout, I was inspired by several articles in magazines, especially Peter Haddock's scenic *Wannetka, Warlock & Western* (Ref. 21). I did not discover John Allen's *Gorre & Daphetid Railroad* (Ref. 22) until the *San Amji* was nearly finished. I now regard John Allen as one of the greatest geniuses of all time in the field of model railwaying. If you want deep inspiration, just look at the stunning pictures of his floor-to-ceiling mountain railway (plus a full city), and then read about the wonderful things that it could do.

Geographical setting: At Holt Junction, somewhere in the Allegheny Mountains, an industrial 'short line' makes a double junction with the Pennsylvania Railroad:

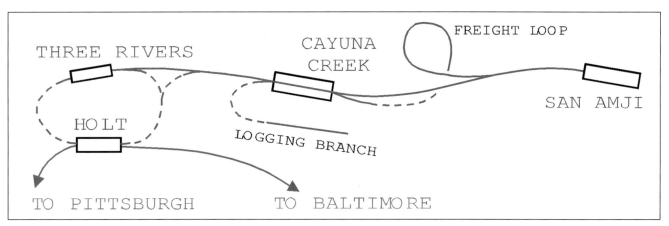

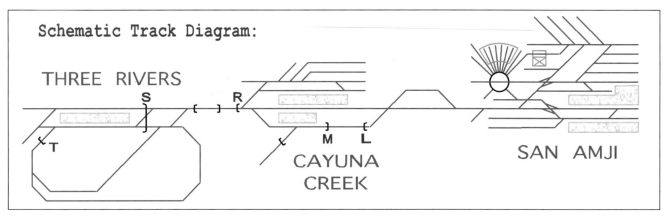

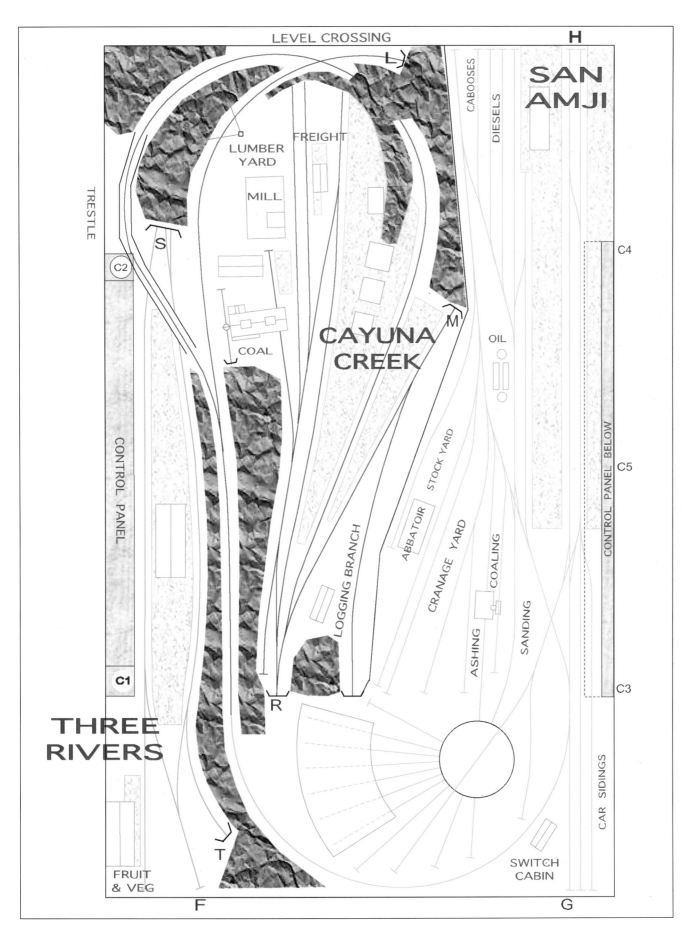

LEVEL CROSSING

H

L

SAN
AMJI

CABOOSES

DIESELS

TRESTLE

LUMBER
YARD

FREIGHT

MILL

C2

S

C4

COAL

M

CAYUNA
CREEK

OIL

CONTROL PANEL

C5

STOCK YARD

ABBATOIR

LOGGING BRANCH

CRANAGE YARD

COALING

CONTROL PANEL BELOW

C1

ASHING

SANDING

C3

THREE
RIVERS

R

CAR SIDINGS

T

SWITCH
CABIN

FRUIT
& VEG

F

G

Design features:
- A compact, semi-portable layout on three levels, with access on all sides.
- Three interlocking stations on different levels, connected by ovals and S-bends.
- Two open-plan control panels built into the main baseboard.
- Four tunnels, requiring electronic track-cleaners and train detectors.

Operation: The railway is set in the post-war period with a mix of steam and diesel traction. The locomotives and rolling stock are leased or bought second-hand from America's major railroads, which explains the colourful mix. San Amji is a commercial town of some importance, with daily through-services to both Pittsburgh and Baltimore. Trains generally comprise six 'heavyweights' including a baggage car at the front and an observation car at the rear (which has to be reversed on the San Amji turntable).

Services start or finish at San Amji, with a choice of passing routes to Cayuna Creek – passenger trains usually taking the trestle bridge while freight takes the tipping-bank above the lumber yard. The simplest routing is out and back via all stations and the hidden reversing loop. Bi-directional diesels may alternatively terminate in a bay at Three Rivers or Cayuna, with the loco running round. A further option is to terminate in Cayuna Creek bay and then to exchange locomotives with a second train terminating at Three Rivers.

There are both through freight trains and 'peddlers' for local industries: ground crops at Three Rivers; cattle and a refrigeration plant at San Amji; a coal mine at Cayuna Creek; lumber from the branch (a short hidden siding); and a timber mill at Cayuna. There is also a small power plant at Cayuna, supplying electricity to the mill. Entry to the coal mine is by an adit (inclined tunnel) which has a (non-operating) narrow gauge railway. There are exchanges of open coal wagons at San Amji MPD where locomotive movements are prolific.

Sections of tunnel are open to view on the end curves and behind the San Amji control panel. Together with the level crossing at the top end, the overall effect of multifarious movements can be enthralling. There are operating restrictions, however, due to the incompatibility of different manufacturers' products concerning couplings, wheels, points and certain motors on feedback control. My track is Peco and points are by Peco, Roco and Shinohara. Locomotives and rolling stock are a mix of American, Japanese and Eastern European manufacture.

Control principles: Two elongated control panels of

Cayuna Creek has the aura of the Wild West. A lumber train pauses on the tip above the timber mill. Ready to depart is a wagon of machined timber and a coal train by the mine. There is little activity at the general goods depot but a local passenger train has just arrived in the terminal platform.

The turntable at San Amji has three approach tracks and eleven storage sidings. The main line threads its way between a track maintenance siding and the switch cabin and disappears behind the roundhouse, far water tower and boiler house chimney. A second water tower serves the locomotive headshunt, bottom left.

A side view across San Amji shows the refrigeration factory (white), general freight yard and coaling tower (centre), the stock yard (left middle) and the MPD (right). In the foreground, a Southern diesel heads a train of reefers out of Cayuna Creek past the water tower and tunnel portal of the logging branch.

varnished mahogany are integral with the main baseboard – one below San Amji and the other alongside Three Rivers (see photograph, opposite). Each has a mimic track diagram made of coloured Dymo tape. Three-position rocker switches (centre off) are set into the mimic diagrams, giving a choice of two cab controllers – left and right. There are five feedback controllers:

- C1 (fixed) – used mainly for Three Rivers and the reversing loop.
- C2 (fixed) – used mainly for Cayuna Creek.
- C3 (wandering lead) – used mainly for San Amji yard.
- C4 (wandering lead) – used mainly for San Amji station and the main line.
- C5 (fixed in the centre of the San Amji board) – used mainly for turntable operation.

An override switch allows C4 to take over the entire layout – this is intended for visitors standing at the top end. A second switch transfers this facility to C5 – a safety feature to guard against careless driving by visitors.

Point operation is manual wherever possible, using local levers. Solenoids are used for unreachable points and for pairs of facing points, energised by flash switches installed on the mimic diagrams. Pairs of facing points at San Amji have a miniature slide switch, connected mechanically to the master and electrically to the slave. All the double-slip points are slaves. For reliability, I have added micro-switches to all point solenoids.

The two points of the reversing loop are operated by a three-position rotary switch (centre off) which also changes the polarity of the power supply to that loop. Siding isolation is mainly by point position, plus push-buttons for certain siding ends.

Uncoupling is mostly manual, using a hooked rod or Peco uncoupling ramps. At Cayuna Creek, which is unreachable, I added solenoids to these ramps, energised by push-buttons on the mimic diagram. Unfortunately, they tend to launch rolling stock into orbit, so I have made a start to convert all stock to electro-magnetic uncoupling, adding steel pins to the standard couplings.

Multi-pin plugs and sockets connect the four baseboards electrically. San Amji has the largest connector with 49 pins. I motorised the Arnold turntable with a Lego motor and gearing, driving a girth gear made from bent segments of Lego rack which are fixed with Araldite to a plastic disc. Power supply to the turntable sidings is via reed switches activated by two small magnets which rotate on the disc.

The tunnels have photocell train detectors, activated by beamed torch bulbs to illuminate LEDs on the mimic diagrams. Encouraged by glowing reports in the model railway press, I installed two electronic track-cleaners for the tunnels, but these proved to be incompatible with my feedback controllers. The subsidiary baseboards must therefore be removed for tunnel track-cleaning.

The grey turntable motor (with the foam spring removed), plastic gearing, the green disc, a bank of reed switches and associated wiring. I used mostly ribbon wiring held by drawing pins to the baseboard undersides.

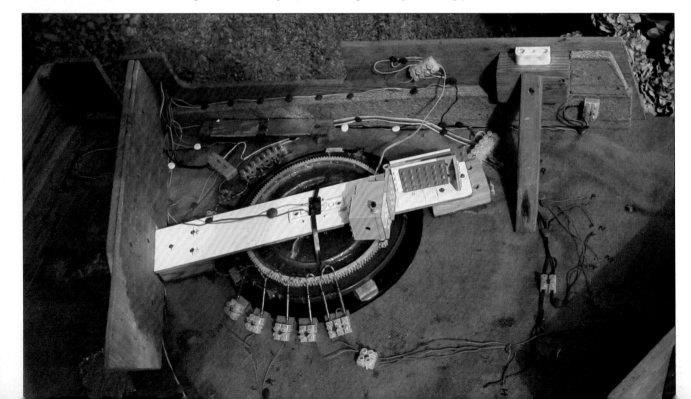

Although this has marred operation and deterred use of the railway, it remains a fine scenic spectacle.

Scenery and accessories:
Scenery is built around slivers of cork bark purchased at exhibitions. At first, I set the cork into chicken-wire-and-Polyfilla hillsides, as seen in the photograph below. The Polyfilla proved to be rather heavy, however, so I later glued the cork to blocks of balsa, with gaps filled with sponge scrub, plastic rocks and proprietary trees. There are no signals as yet but lines of telegraph poles provide a nice finishing touch, together with road vehicles, huts, water towers, signalboxes, platform furniture, people, horses and cattle.

I derived much satisfaction from scratch-building the trestle, Three Rivers station building, the stock yard and several cranes and water towers. Most of the buildings, however, are made from wooden or plastic kits supplied by US, UK and Continental manufacturers. The wooden kits were particularly detailed and intricate, especially the coaling tower and the 'combination town depot' at San Amji.

Locomotives and rolling stock:
All ready-to-run, the photograph on page 101 shows a selection. Outlines and finishes are excellent but most of the locomotives require regular attention to brushes, magnets or 'motion' (testing one's eyesight). One

diesel raises its leading wheels and tends to derail on points. So the stud is a mixed bunch in terms of reliability.

Construction: The main baseboard spans the width of our garage, supported on four slotted wooden posts screwed to the garage walls. It is an open frame of three longitudinal and six cross beams of deal, screwed and glued together. Strengthened by areas of chipboard, the frame was pre-stressed by screwing the chipboard into place with the frame bent upwards. This up-bending helps to cancel the sag when the weights of two control panels and three subsidiary baseboards are added.

Three subsidiary baseboards

A Baltimore & Ohio diesel locomotive heads a train of Pennsylvania 'heavyweights' out of Three Rivers while a Chippewa Pacific approaches on the trestle. The industries and town buildings of Cayuna Creek are visible beyond. On the mahogany control panel can be seen the Dymo tape which mimics Cayuna Creek, together with large rocker-type section switches, throw-type flash point switches and colour-coded push-buttons for the uncoupler solenoids. Feed-back controller C2 is at the end, operating left, centre-off and right. The switch settings show that Cayuna main platform (red) is selected to C1 while the freight yard (green) is switched 'off'. In operation, there are frequent cab calls of 'Give me green' or 'I'm taking pink', referring to section colours.

are fixed to the main baseboard by Conti-joins. They comprise a deal underframe with a full surface of Sundeala board - this is much lighter than chipboard and takes pins, screws, drill bits and pencil marks so much better. Each subsidiary baseboard can be lifted by two persons but the main baseboard requires four people for safe lifting. The railway is semi-transportable (like a mobile home), so is unlikely to be seen at exhibitions. Fully assembled, dimensions are 2.4m by 1.4m by 0.3m tall (to the top of the coaling tower).

The garage location is ideal for segregating the railway from domestic activities, also for the freedom to make a mess on the floor and for having all tools ready to hand. The main disadvantages are dirt, cobwebs and condensation between operating sessions.

Construction of the main baseboard showing the ovals and the hidden S-shape reversing loop.

All four baseboards during early construction, showing Three Rivers (left), Cayuna Creek (centre), the MPD and turntable hole (right) and San Amji (top).

The colourful San Amji terminus is separated from Cayuna Creek by a sylvan hillside. The two central main line passenger tracks are suitable for extension (see Railway No. 9). There is a bay platform, a baggage platform and five sidings for diesel and caboose storage. Centre-scene are the diesel storage and fuelling points. Freight sidings peel off to the left. The control panel shows section switches, point switches and push-buttons to energise siding ends. The tunnel main line rises on a ramp just behind the control panel and there is a Velcro pad at the far end to hold the wandering-lead controller C4. (Howard Warren)

9

Extensions to the San Amji Railroad

Summary description: At the top end of Layout No. 8, a scenic out-and-back loop runs through a major port and township, connected to San Amji via a high-level bridge (H). At the bottom end, a city terminus is connected via spirals and bridges to both San Amji (G) and Three Rivers (F). The city also incorporates an inter-urban streetcar system.

Inspiration: San Amji terminus was designed for possible extension to become a through-station. The new port, city and streetcars were all inspired by John Allen's *Gorre & Daphetid Railroad* (Ref. 22). The whole-train turntable was inspired by Peter Denny's hidden turntable (representing Quainton Road) on his *Buckingham Great Central* line (Ref. 23), but its application to a whole-station is my own idea. The destination Desire is from the Marlon Brando film.

Design features: The top-end extension (right) comprises a double-track main line spiralling down to a simple loop through the port with freight sidings at the quay. This concept is similar to that of the garden loop of Layout No. 2, *The Highland Garden Railway*. The bottom-end extension, on the other hand (opposite page), has some novel design features as follows:
- A symmetric whole-station turntable, simplifying the train reversal procedure.

- The sharing of certain station tracks with the streetcar system.

Control principles: There are two additional cab controllers at the top end and three at the bottom end, together with associated section and override switches. The streetcars have dummy pick-up pantographs. Most of the additional points are manual. Communication between the four control zones is by headphone. The three new bridges carry control cabling.

Operation: The top-end extension simplifies operation by allowing continuous running in dumb bell mode. The entire railway can then be operated by just three people – located respectively at Three Rivers, San Amji and Port Allenby – who control passing movements and make occasional whole-train exchanges from the sidings. If the bottom extension is then added, two additional operators are needed at Engage City, respectively for mainline trains and the streetcars. For full operation of all stations and yards, eight operators are needed (plus reserves).

Construction: A clubroom is needed, measuring some 10m by

3.5m for N gauge. Three braced frames support the three (immoveable) railway systems from the floor, leaving two deep chasms, about 0.7m wide, crossed by three showpiece bridges. With construction in three phases, the entire layout could take some ten to twenty years to complete.

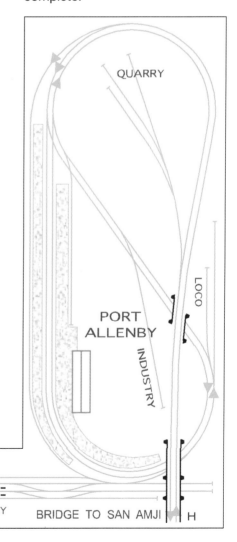

QUARRY

PORT ALLENBY

LOCO

INDUSTRY

CRANES   QUAY   BRIDGE TO SAN AMJI   H

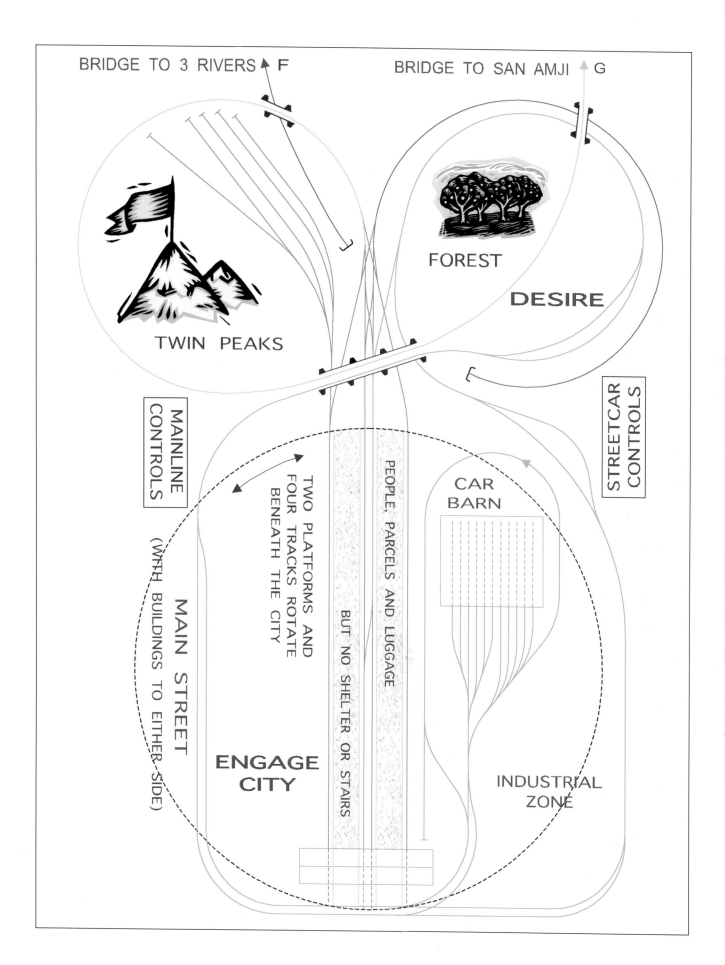

BRIDGE TO 3 RIVERS ↑ F

BRIDGE TO SAN AMJI ↑ G

TWIN PEAKS

FOREST

DESIRE

MAINLINE CONTROLS

STREETCAR CONTROLS

CAR BARN

PEOPLE, PARCELS AND LUGGAGE

BUT NO SHELTER OR STAIRS

TWO PLATFORMS AND FOUR TRACKS ROTATE BENEATH THE CITY

MAIN STREET (WITH BUILDINGS TO EITHER SIDE)

ENGAGE CITY

INDUSTRIAL ZONE

41

10

Severn & Dorset Garden Railway

Summary description: A convoluted oval in the garden and a double oval in a purpose-built shed, to be operated singly or together. Also reversing loops, several branches and a port with a real pond and boats.

Inspiration: During the winter of 1973-74, the coal and oil crises resulted, among other things, in the three-day week, the fall of the Heath government and car-sharing to work. Sharing with three local colleagues, I used to wait at the end of my road for up to ten minutes on about three mornings per week. The bungalow on the corner was surrounded by a simple but spacious garden, open to view across a dry-stone wall and crying out for an O gauge model railway. I duly obliged with a plan that would take some ten years to complete. The SR's Wenfordbridge line and the real Leckhampton line inspired the quarry branch. Articles in August editions of *Railway Modeller* inspired the pond while John Allen's train ferry (Ref. 22) inspired the Sharpness dock development.

Historical setting: Victorian parliament took many opportunities to promote railway competition. A good example is the Birmingham line to Bristol and Bath which was awarded to the Midland Railway. A further incursion into GWR territory was

the Somerset & Dorset line which became Midland and LSWR Joint. A prime cross-country route was thereby created from Poole to the Midlands and the North, used mainly for holiday traffic to the Bournemouth area but also picking up traffic from industries along the route. Keeping to the basic S&D concept, I upgraded Poole to a cross-channel port and re-routed the line through Bristol Eastville and Thornbury. Sharpness became a through-station with a train-carrying ferry to Lydney where an invented independent line runs to South Wales. The layout thereby offers a new railway service from Normandy to South Wales. Although far-fetched commercially, such a line makes for a great model railway.

Design features:
- A full garden take-over in O gauge but not interfering with normal access to the house and garage.
- A secure workshop-cum-storeroom built alongside the garage and leading to the new shed at the rear for bad-weather operation.
- An indoor section suitable for continuous test running or end-to-end operation.
- Whole-train storage sidings under the indoor terminus.
- A 'sociable' garden section in full public view (in an area of comparatively low risk of vandalism).

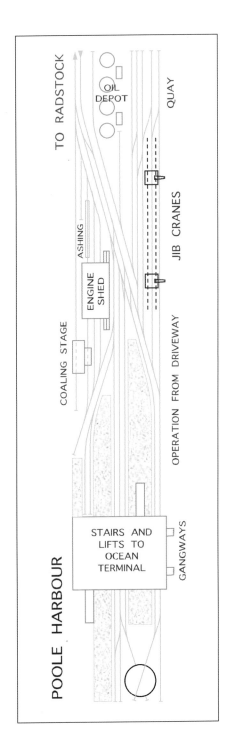

TO RADSTOCK · OIL DEPOT · QUAY · ASHING · JIB CRANES · ENGINE SHED · COALING STAGE · OPERATION FROM DRIVEWAY · STAIRS AND LIFTS TO OCEAN TERMINAL · GANGWAYS · POOLE HARBOUR

- The stone wall is rebuilt at the front and side of the property, with tracks laid upon, below (at the front) and through it (see scale plan, bottom-right).
- The garden section incorporates a long, continuous run.
- Full landscaping is centred upon a spectacular dockland pond with live whales and a radio-controlled tug.

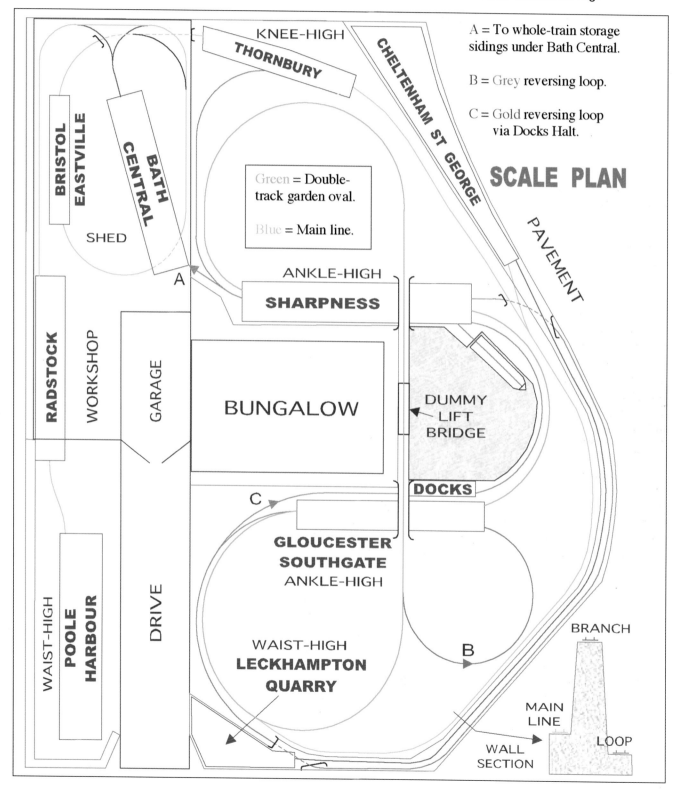

A = To whole-train storage sidings under Bath Central.

B = Grey reversing loop.

C = Gold reversing loop via Docks Halt.

SCALE PLAN

KNEE-HIGH
THORNBURY

CHELTENHAM ST GEORGE

PAVEMENT

BRISTOL EASTVILLE

BATH CENTRAL

SHED

Green = Double-track garden oval.

Blue = Main line.

ANKLE-HIGH
SHARPNESS

A

RADSTOCK

WORKSHOP

GARAGE

BUNGALOW

DUMMY LIFT BRIDGE

DOCKS

C

GLOUCESTER SOUTHGATE
ANKLE-HIGH

WAIST-HIGH
POOLE HARBOUR

DRIVE

WAIST-HIGH
LECKHAMPTON QUARRY

B

BRANCH

MAIN LINE

WALL SECTION

LOOP

Control principles:
- Cab controllers for the indoor section, with switching panels alongside Radstock, Bristol and Bath.
- Wandering-lead cab controllers

for Poole, Cheltenham and Leckhampton, connected to a lockable, weather-proof control cubicle below each station.
- Wandering-lead cab controllers for the garden oval (including

Gloucester and Sharpness) supplied from a switching panel located in a room of the bungalow where the Fat Controller lives.
- The Thin Controller lives in the

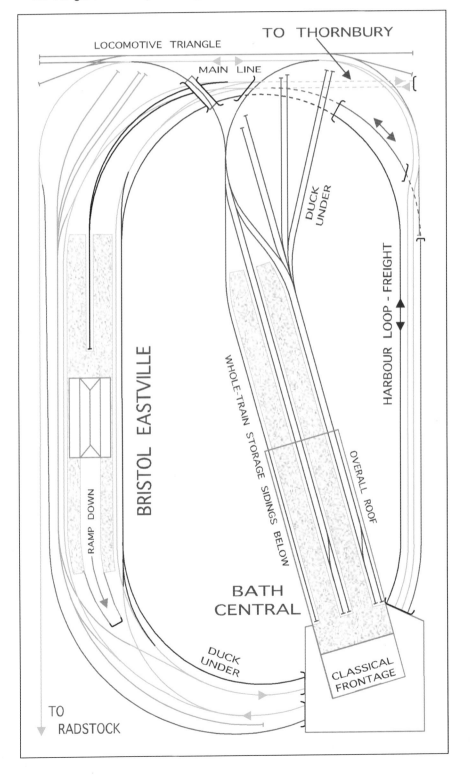

shed. Most through-trains stop at Thornbury for transfer between the two divisions.

- Radstock is used similarly for transfers to and from Poole.
- Communication is by voice, bell and telephone.

Indoor operation:

(Prevalent in winter and in wet weather, also useful for test runs.)

- Tender engine fast passenger trains operate out and back from Bath.
- Push-pull services run between Bath and Bristol bay.
- Tank engine passenger trains operate end to end between Radstock and Bath. In dry, cold conditions, the service can be extended to Thornbury (controlled remotely from the shed).
- Freight trains run between all stations.

Full operation:

- Normandy–South Wales boat trains operate out and back from Poole to Sharpness, including the 'Wessex Wayfarer', the 'Pullman Conqueror', the 'Trans-Wessex Express', and fitted freights.
- SR/LMS local passenger trains operate end to end between Poole and Bath.
- GWR passenger trains operate out and back from Cheltenham, looping as far as Thornbury.
- Push-pull trains run between Sharpness (north bay) and Thornbury via Docks Halt.
- Limestone trains run between Leckhampton and Cheltenham, often with a workmens' coach.
- Pick-up freight trains call twice-daily at all main stations.
- Specialised freight trains operate periodically out of: Poole (oil), Radstock (coal), Cheltenham (limestone), Gloucester (timber), and Sharpness (grain).

Construction: The site measures approximately 50m by 40m. Ideally, the Fat Controller wins a fortune on the National Lottery to establish an S&D Trust to perpetuate the model railway on this site. The bungalow then becomes a hostel for visiting builders, landscape gardeners, modellers, operators and other specialists working to a ten-year initial programme of construction. Since gardens and model railways alike are never truly 'finished', refinements and improvements could go on for decades.

Details of garden stations (not to scale) are shown below.

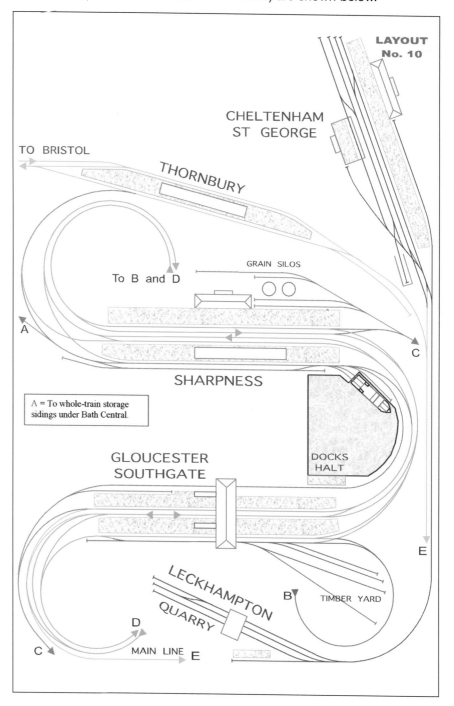

11

The Star Rabbit Warren

Summary description: A star-shape reversing loop with tunnels and a high-level terminus, particularly suitable for N gauge.

Inspiration: A general source of inspiration is a series of 1960s booklets of track plans by Peco Publications (Ref. 24). The one on *Larger Layouts* is particularly good, showing not only some elaborate plans but a spectacular cover photograph of the docks, lifting bridge and scenic backdrop of Jeff Colledge's *North Midland Railway*. I was further inspired by some novel long-train layout ideas published in *Railway Modeller* when coarse-scale N gauge took off in the late 1960s. We are indebted to Cyril Freezer, renowned editor, author and raconteur, who prepared the booklets and many of the plans. Peninsular baseboards feature in some of his N gauge designs, including three peninsulas in parallel to create an E-shape (Ref. 25). My new development is to use three such peninsulas in a 3 x 120° star-shape.

Design features:
- A dominant terminus, occupying the top level of all three prongs of the star, with generous passenger platforms, parcels and goods loading, a carriage shed and a full MPD.
- A double-track main line with a tunnel, through-station and a coal mine, factory or quarry.
- Two convoluted reversing loops with tunnels.

- Three-point turns for locomotives at the terminus, needing no turntable.
- All-round viewing, offering different perspectives of multifarious movements.

Control principles: Using cab control, the main switching panel is mounted on the face of the four-storey station building at the bottom of the plan. From here, the Traffic Master operates main line points and section switches for the cab drivers with wandering leads around the layout. There are LEDs and mirrors for the unsighted tracks. The terminus signalman sits at the top end with his own switching panel. In full operation, up to eight operators are kept busy. Automatic operation could also be developed, by using the three-train regime described below.

Operation:
- Three-train automatic operation has one train on each main line (red and blue) while a third is held on a reversing loop (gold or pink). Trains then transfer in sequence to the reversing loops and to the terminus.
- With additional operators available, additional trains use the colliery loop and both blue tracks at the through-station (with van shunting into the blue bay).
- Push-pull/EMU/DMU services can also be added, terminating in the through-station (red) bay.
- The terminus provides the main

operating spectacle, with continual movement of locomotives, empty stock, parcels vans, fuel and goods wagons.

Construction: The layout measures 4m by 4m in N gauge, to which at least 0.6m must be added all round for access, control and viewing. It is intended as a permanent club layout, taking five to ten years to complete. Constructed on a main frame of timber or Dexion, the main lines, reversing loops and switching panels are permanently fixed. The terminus, on the other hand, is built off-stage on four sub-baseboards which are removable for occasional maintenance, modification and access to the tunnels. Indeed, the terminus could be taken to exhibitions, operating end to end to a simple storage yard.

Geometry: I have never seen a star-shaped model railway for real. Most portable layouts are rectangular while permanent layouts are tailored to fit the space available. Circular layouts are rare. Hamleys toyshop in London used to have an intriguing circular layout around the first-floor balcony of the grand stairwell, with Fleischmann tracks criss-crossing in a giant Perspex-covered ellipse. When the store was rebuilt in the 1980s, the stairwell and HO railway had to go, but a new G gauge track was installed just below the ceiling on the ground floor.

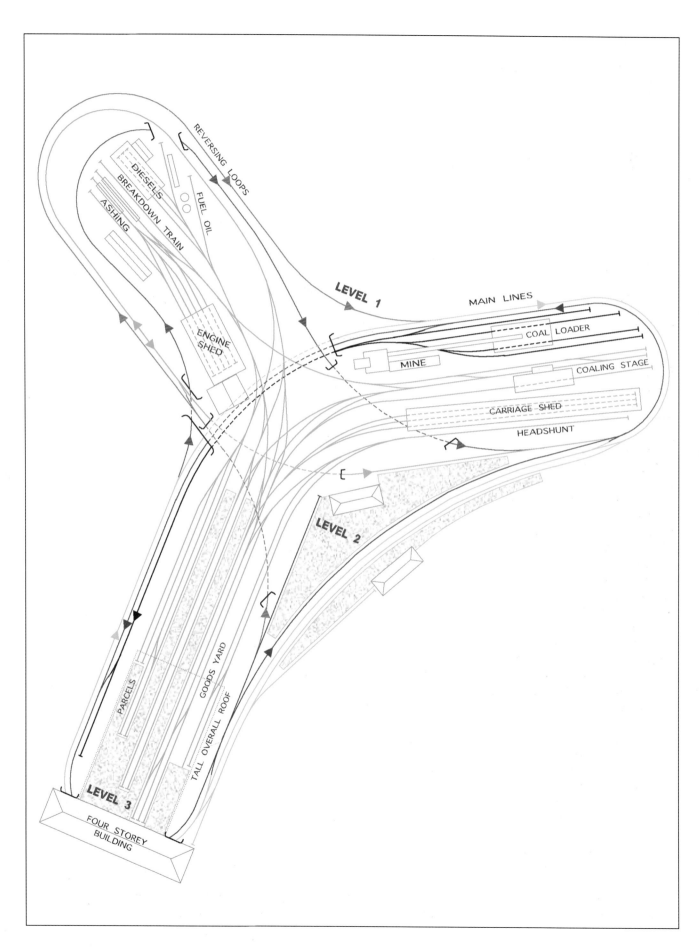

REVERSING LOOPS

DIESELS

BREAKDOWN TRAIN

ASHING

FUEL OIL

ENGINE SHED

LEVEL 1

MAIN LINES

COAL LOADER

MINE

COALING STAGE

CARRIAGE SHED

HEADSHUNT

LEVEL 2

PARCELS

GOODS YARD

TALL OVERALL ROOF

LEVEL 3

FOUR STOREY BUILDING

12

Bodmin Branch Railways

Summary description: A 4mm multi-level complex of ovals, branch lines and an out-and-back loop, representing the LSWR and GWR steam railways in and around the Camel and Fowey valleys.

Inspiration: Many holidays enjoyed around Padstow, Bodmin and Fowey during 1959-2002. The multi-level design concept was greatly inspired by Keith Ladbury's *GWR and LMS Lines* (Ref. 26).

Historical setting: The Bodmin & Wadebridge Railway was one of

Britain's earliest steam lines, opening in 1834 and taken over by the LSWR in 1847. Adjacent lines grew piecemeal, eventually connecting with the GWR in 1887 and with the LSWR proper in 1895. Quarries at Wenfordbridge first produced china clay in 1862 and this became the principal freight commodity. The clay was exported first from Wadebridge and then from Fowey, the latter requiring train reversals at Boscarne, Bodmin General and Bodmin Road. Today, Wenfordbridge, Wadebridge and Padstow are long closed but

steam can still be enjoyed on the preserved lines between Boscarne and Bodmin Road (now called Parkway). The Fowey branch remains open for china clay trains from the area north-west of St Austell (see photographs on page 52). Fowey was once bi-directional, with a second branch running to St Blazey and Newquay (with china clay branches at Bugle and St Dennis). The Newquay branch today carries passenger traffic from Par, but the old trackbed from Par Sands to Fowey now carries china clay in road lorries.

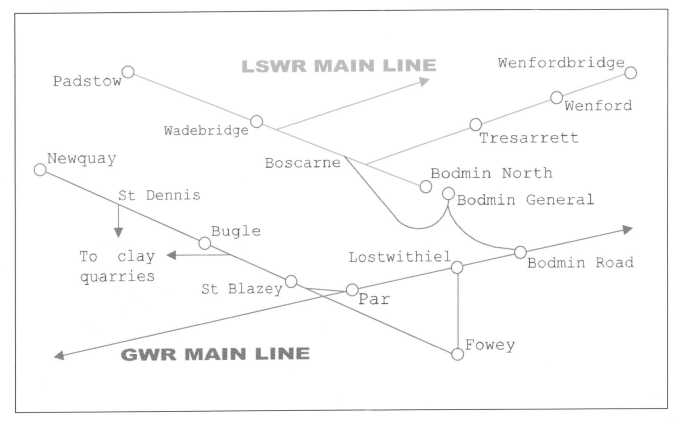

Design and Construction: The classic way to accommodate so many stations and junctions is on multiple levels. The section (right) shows the various baseboards. They are bracketed to the walls of two rooms, rising from near floor-level to about chest-high. Each level would be individually lit, using strip lights fixed to the baseboard above. Access is via two steep ladders (with suitable safety rails), either through the floor or through the ceiling. The plan measures 5.5m by 6m overall in 4mm scale. This club project would take some five to ten years to build. The design lends itself to modular construction, with separate teams building individual stations off-site to fine-scale standards. Conceptual station layouts are drawn overleaf, broadly representing their prototypes. Section control is appropriate, with changeover switches at all the main stations.

Operation: (Any or all of the following services according to the number of operators available.)

- LSWR main line passenger and freight trains run out and back from Padstow via the green loop.
- LSWR local passenger and freight trains run end to end between Padstow and Bodmin North.
- GWR local passenger trains run between Wadebridge, Bodmin General and Bodmin Road.
- GWR main line passenger and freight trains run on the double-track oval via Bodmin Road.
- LSWR well-tanks head china clay and general freight trains

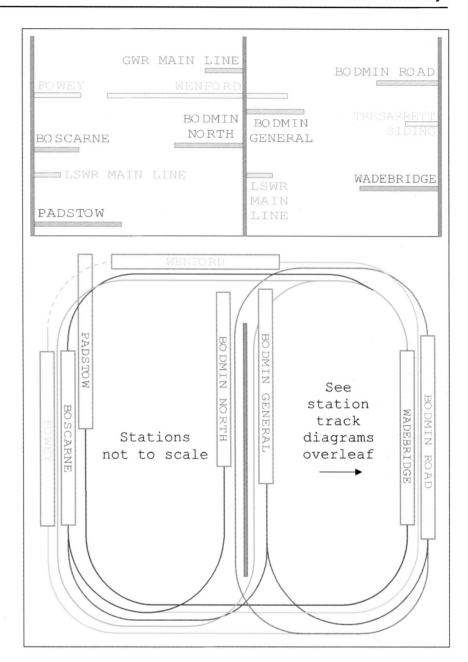

between Boscarne and Wenfordbridge.
- GWR tanks head china clay trains from Boscarne to Fowey, also general freight trains from Bodmin Road.
- A GWR motor-train operates between Fowey and Bodmin Road.

- China clay trains are exchanged surreptitiously between Wenford and Fowey. By this means, one full clay train always runs clockwise and one empty train anticlockwise, giving the impression of a constant flow of the product.

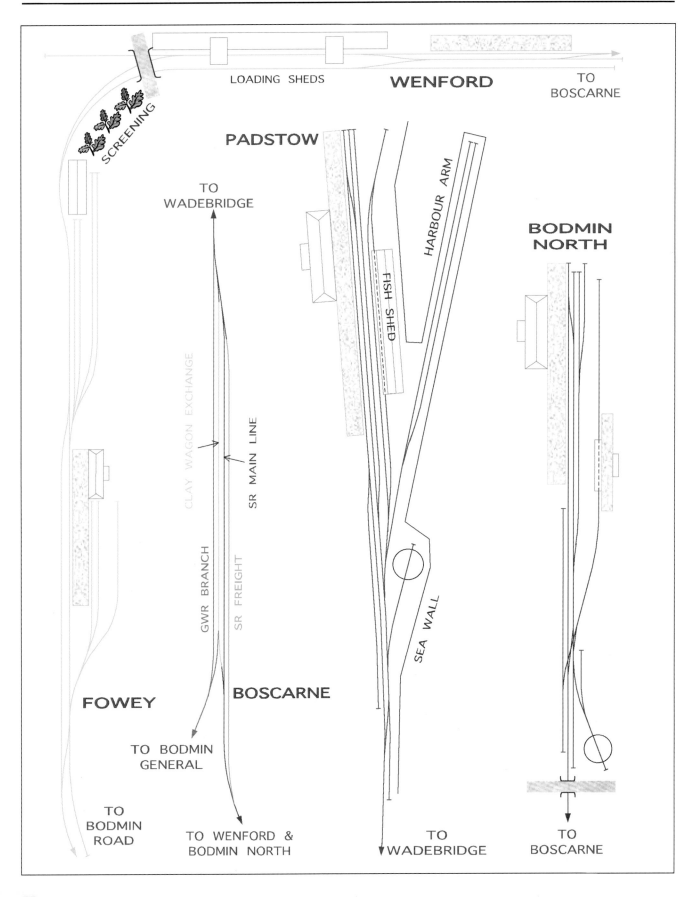

LOADING SHEDS

WENFORD

TO BOSCARNE

SCREENING

PADSTOW

TO WADEBRIDGE

HARBOUR ARM

BODMIN NORTH

FISH SHED

CLAY WAGON EXCHANGE

SR MAIN LINE

GWR BRANCH

SR FREIGHT

SEA WALL

FOWEY

BOSCARNE

TO BODMIN GENERAL

TO BODMIN ROAD

TO WENFORD & BODMIN NORTH

TO WADEBRIDGE

TO BOSCARNE

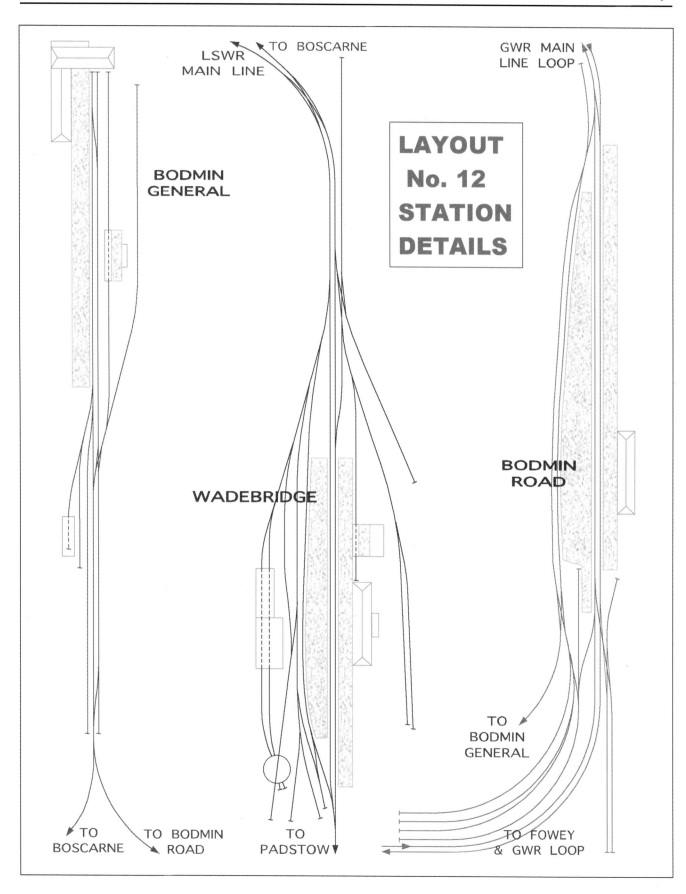

TO BOSCARNE

LSWR
MAIN LINE

GWR MAIN
LINE LOOP

BODMIN
GENERAL

LAYOUT
No. 12
STATION
DETAILS

BODMIN
ROAD

WADEBRIDGE

TO
BODMIN
GENERAL

TO
BOSCARNE

TO BODMIN
ROAD

TO
PADSTOW

TO FOWEY
& GWR LOOP

Photographs relating to Layout No.12 show contrasting styles of locomotives and clay wagons. Above: In 1959, on the Wenfordbridge branch near Boscarne, LSWR well-tank No. 30585 emerges into sunshine from East Wood, with a train of loaded clay wagons. The open wagons are five-plank wooden with three-link couplings, covered with tarpaulins for weather protection. Below: In 2002, EWS Class 66 diesel locomotive No. 66125 approaches Fowey with a train of loaded hoppers from the clay mining area north-west of St Austell, having reversed at Lostwithiel. The steel wagons are enclosed and fitted with continuous braking.

At the 2002 Mendip Exhibition, 'Canalside' is a fine example of an OO gauge portable scenic layout. Built over 2½ years by Andy Jones, Hughie Jones, Bill Brown and Mike Mears of the Burnham & District MRC, this simple oval has just four points on the viewing side. The emphasis is upon scenery, with the 'set' of the canal below the central bridge breaking up the symmetry. Note the working signals, dummy point rodding and beautifully finished ballast and trees. For night operation, lights can be seen in the signalbox and from lamps on the platforms, lock sides and canal basin (out of shot, bottom left).

13

Liverpool & Binns Road

Summary description: A large L-shape Hornby Dublo layout comprising a three-track oval with a reversing loop, a through-station and a terminus. It offers intensive services with a great variety of train types, shunting and locomotive movements, suitable for exhibitions.

Inspiration: A Hornby Dublo layout put together for a parents' day exhibition at my secondary school. I was much impressed by passing trains of six coaches and by the terminus located off-stage in the corridor, making a large L-shape. I was less impressed by operational limitations due to the lack of reversing facilities or a turntable. Decades later, inspired by born-again Hornby Dublo layouts in magazines and at exhibitions, I added a reversing loop, two goods yards, an MPD and an end-of-platform turntable. Inspirations for the turntable location were two compact LCDR termini - Ramsgate Harbour which closed in 1926 - and Crystal Palace high-level which closed in

1955 (see also Layout No. 22).

A general inspiration for all HD layouts is Michael Foster's encyclopaedic book *Hornby Dublo Trains* (Ref. 27). Beautifully illustrated, it is a complete history and catalogue of three Hornby systems (3-rail OO, 2-rail OO and French AcHO) covering track, locomotives, rolling stock and accessories.

Historical background:
Station names on the model are the works address of Meccano, the former makers of Hornby Dublo. The product was marketed as 'The Perfect Table Railway', an epitaph which remains as true today as in the late 1930s. The 3-rail steel track looked and felt good and the locomotives were wonderful - my own HD locomotives required no maintenance or repairs during five years of regular use (1950-55). Even the short tin-plate coaches with painted windows – crude by modern standards – were a delight to own. Hornby Dublo collectors make regular

appearances at exhibitions to this day. Their layouts are characteristically compact, as befits a table railway. A fine example is Don and Gloria Hillyar's layout (see page 88).

Design features:
- Single level, suitable for temporary locations on the floor or on tables.
- Track geometry and accessories suitable for 3-rail Hornby Dublo or modern equivalent.
- A three-track simple oval with a through-station.
- A goods yard to be integral with the reversing loop.
- A long, spectacular terminus with an overall roof, goods yard and MPD.
- Two bays and a works halt, suitable for push-pull/EMU/ DMU trains.

Control principles: With so much continuous running envisaged on the ovals, digital control is a possibility. However, HD purists would no doubt opt for the traditional resistance or variable-

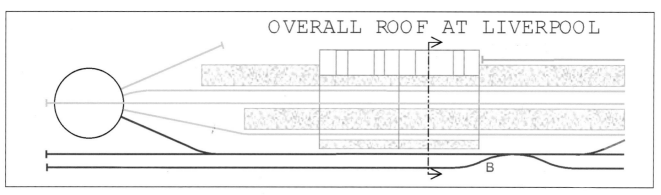

OVERALL ROOF AT LIVERPOOL

transformer controllers. Three people would then operate five electrical sections as follows:

- Two controllers located on the right of the layout plan (Inner and Middle).
- Two controllers located at the inside corner of the L-shape (Outer and Terminus).
- One controller located at the bottom of the plan (Liverpool Yard).

The gold section (bottom right) is supplied via a two-position switch from Terminus or Liverpool Yard. All points and uncouplers are hand operated. Siding isolation is mainly by point position, with some push-buttons for siding ends. At exhibitions, visitors are segregated to the right and bottom of the layout, and are invited to take turns in point operation, shunting and turntable operation at Liverpool Yard.

Operation: Principal passenger trains depart from the three long platforms at Liverpool. After stopping at Binns Road middle platform, they proceed to the middle fast line, then take the reversing loop R to the inner oval. Returning via the two crossovers, they are held in the outer oval until a terminal road is free at Liverpool. The locomotive then turns and runs round via the MPD.

General goods trains take a similar route to passenger trains but dwell at Binns Road Yard for shunting. A colourful train of fuel oil tankers makes occasional outings from siding F at Liverpool, also a breakdown train from siding B. Binns Road siding S is also available for whole-train storage – passenger, goods or parcels.

Short push-pull/EMU/DMU trains depart Liverpool bay via Binns Road Outer to Yarde Halt.

They then run to Binns Road middle platform and reverse to Binns Road bay. Finally, they cross back to Binns Road Outer and to the bay at Liverpool.

Construction: Although operationally similar to Layout No. 5, *The Crantock Railway*, construction here is much simpler, being on a single level and requiring only floor space or a group of tables or trestles for temporary exhibition (ideally with a baize cloth). Overall dimensions are 4.2m by 3.7m. Small shelves for the controllers are clamped to the trestles. The main constructional challenge is to package the railway securely in boxes for transportation and storage. Re-assembling the track for an exhibition can be expected to take a couple of hours at least. A sack truck is invaluable.

Accessories: Station platforms, buildings, goods stations and engine shed can be traditional Hornby Dublo, together with a scattering of signals, signalboxes and other minor accessories. Station forecourts and yards can be brought to life by a scattering of Dinky Toys. One can imagine taxis and GPO vans waiting at Liverpool, while saloon cars and a bus might feature at Binns Road. To make a visual break, a custom-built bridge could be built cross the four tracks (top left), leading on to a curved ramp down to Binns Road forecourt, plus a level

crossing to the goods yard (below the R). Like the engine shed and the overall roof, such visual breaks are valuable on small oval layouts as a respite from continuous running. Don Hillyar achieves this with a tunnel at each end of his layout, together with a hidden loop at the back, below the control panel (see photograph on page 88).

14

Putnam Division of the New York Central

Summary description: A double oval around my loft, with three through-stations and two termini.

Inspiration: Ron Edward's *Melford & Tawton* model railway (Ref. 28) comprises a simple oval around his loft with two rival low-level termini (SR and GWR). My large Gloucestershire loft cried out for such a layout, offering an alternative home (dirt and condensation free) for my American N gauge stock of Railway No. 8, the *San Amji*. The geographic setting was inspired generally by articles in *Railroad Model Craftsman* and *Model Railroader*, and specifically by a book - Ref. 29, *The Putnam Division*.

Historical setting: The New York, Boston & Montreal Railroad was like the London Extension of the Great Central – one main line too many! Uncompleted and never economic, it was taken over in 1894 by the New York Central as its Putnam Division, known affectionately as the 'Put'. Most of its 54 miles to Putnam Junction was operated like a single-track branch. Yorktown Heights was one of 30 simple up-country stations with commuter trains. The short spur from Yonkers became a busy electrified (outside third) commuter line into downtown New York. For environmental reasons, only electric trains were allowed into Grand Central Terminal, but there

was cross-platform transfer at High Bridge where the NYC main line ran parallel with the 'Put'. Sedgwick Avenue in the Bronx was the 'Put's modest terminus for steam and diesel trains, with surface connection to the Interborough Rapid Transit (subway). Sadly, the 'Put' closed to passengers in 1958 and to all traffic in 1977. The model is set the 1930s with a locomotive mix of steam and America's very first diesels, interspersed with three-car Yonkers EMUs and off-peak gas-electric cars on the main line (unelectrified).

Design, operation and control: The railway is intended for long

RED = TOP LEVEL

VAN CORTLANDT

BLUE = BOTTOM LEVEL

LOCOS

YORKTOWN HEIGHTS

CRAWL UNDER →

HOUSEHOLD STORAGE

YONKERS

LADDER SPACE

HATCH

FREIGHT YARD

GREEN = MIDDLE LEVEL

continuous runs around the double oval, with trains passing at the through-stations and with periodic visits to the termini and the whole-train storage sidings S. There is modest locomotive storage at the two termini.

Using cab control and a mimic switching panel alongside High Bridge, it can be operated by one person or by a group. The pointwork at High Bridge is designed to allow a variety of routes for timetable operation. Yonkers was designed originally with a second spur for in-and-out working, but I prefer greater authenticity with the right-hand spur used only for locomotive turning.

Construction: This a partial take-over of the loft, with household storage below the baseboards and in the left-hand well. The two water tanks are left free for maintenance access. The baseboards are supported on posts from the existing floorboards. The hatch already has a folding ladder and safety railings. New items include wall and ceiling boards, central heating, improved lighting, smoke detectors and fire extinguishers. There are no intermediate trusses, offering a huge space for modelling in N gauge. The layout measures 12.7m by 3.3m, built between longitudinal purlins – see the cross-sectional diagram on page 18. Railway No. 28, *The Chicago & Western*, makes even greater use of this loft space for modelling.

Traffic on the 'Put':
- Through freight to Boston.
- Oversize freight to Albany (single track, no tunnels).
- Local factory freight.
- Local iron ore.
- EMUs to Yonkers.
- Gas-electric cars.
- Passenger steam to Brewster (just past Putnam Junction).

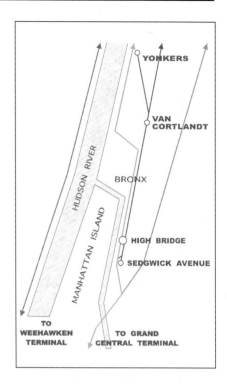

New York Central Lines:

Pink	West Shore Line to Albany
Green	Main Line to Chicago
Red	Putnam Division
Gold	Harlem Division to Albany

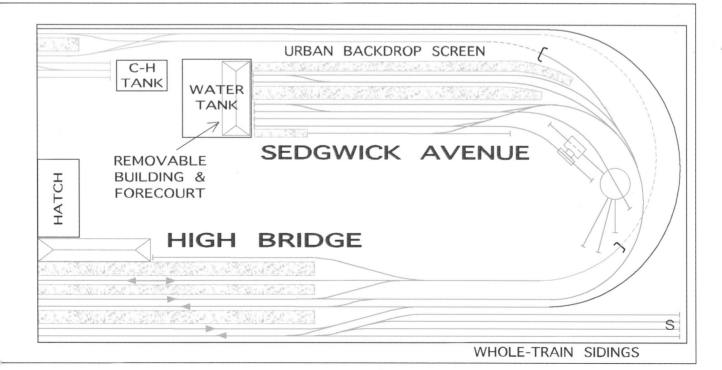

15

The Northumbria Garden Railway

Summary description: A reversing loop with two branch lines, laid in my garden and in a converted cowshed.

Inspiration: We have a large garden in the Cotswolds, which was once part of a smallholding. The former cowshed stands just beyond our fence and could be converted into a perfect model railway den. Alas, my offer to buy it was rejected, but not before I had designed a perfect O gauge layout to fit both the shed and the periphery of our garden. The principal station (inside the shed) was inspired by three model through-stations, each having a long goods yard and an MPD:

- Barrie Walls's *Wallsea Main* (Ref. 30), a fine-scale portable layout in O gauge.
- The Manchester Model Railway Society's *Wheatstone Bridge* (Ref. 31), modelled in OO gauge.
- Keith Robins's *Rhosteigne* (Ref. 32), a colourful loft layout nicely finished in N gauge.

I was further inspired by two O gauge garden railways which have a principal station in a large shed: Don Neale's *Kirtley* (Ref. 33); and G. E. Bigmore's *Bigston to Archway* (Ref. 34). A Northumbrian setting was chosen to fit the character of the line - a mix of express trains, coastal coal trains and mineral and agricultural traffic into the hills.

Back garden: Hexham is a busy country town with the following rail traffic:

- Newcastle-Carlisle through trains which sometimes stop at Hexham.
- Morpeth suburban passenger trains terminate in Platform 4.
- Hexham cattle trains, generally running on the (red) main line.
- Pick-up freight trains visit Hexham and Allendale yards.
- The push-pull 'Allendale Billy'.

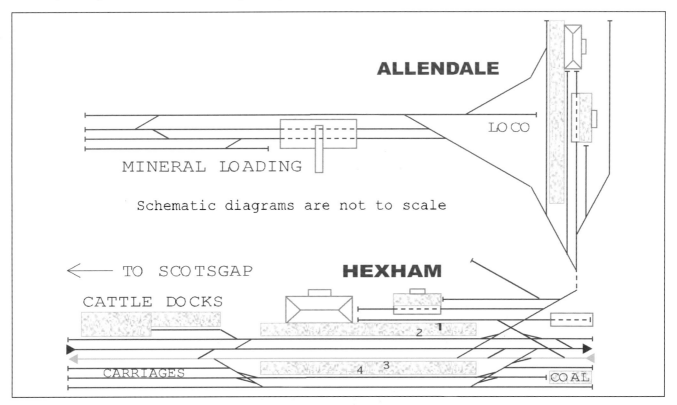

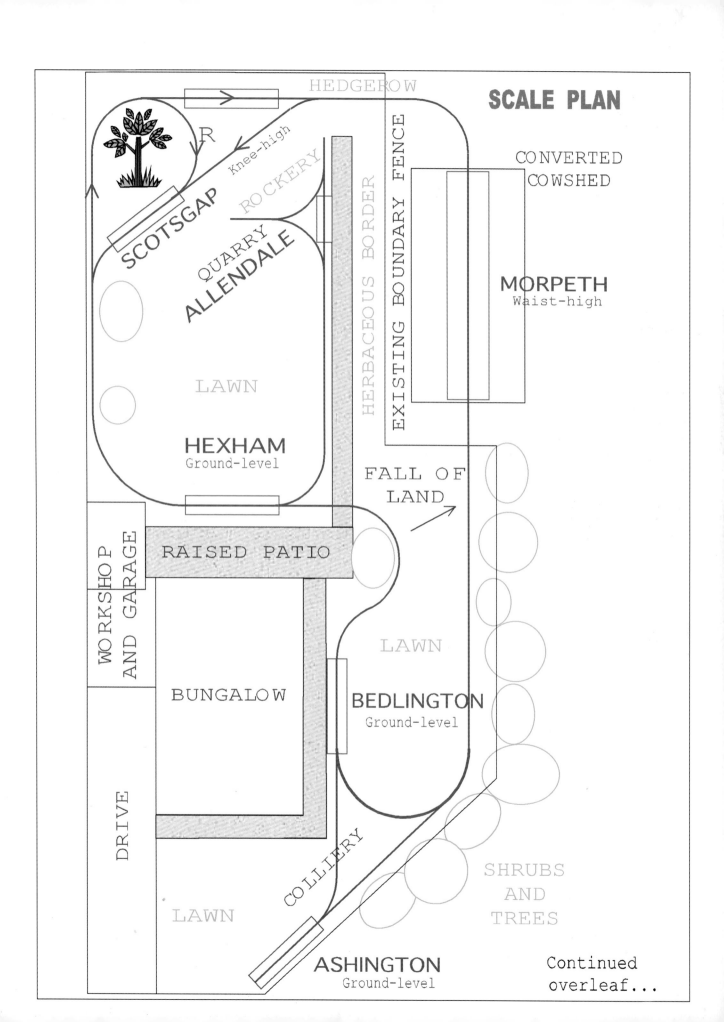

SCALE PLAN

HEDGEROW

R

Knee-high

SCOTSGAP

ROCKERY

QUARRY
ALLENDALE

HERBACEOUS BORDER

EXISTING BOUNDARY FENCE

CONVERTED
COWSHED

MORPETH
Waist-high

LAWN

HEXHAM
Ground-level

FALL OF
LAND

WORKSHOP
AND GARAGE

RAISED PATIO

BUNGALOW

LAWN

BEDLINGTON
Ground-level

DRIVE

COLLIERY

SHRUBS
AND
TREES

LAWN

ASHINGTON
Ground-level

Continued
overleaf...

- Mineral trains from Allendale run on to the (blue) main line, returning in due course via the reversing loop R.
- Enthusiasts' specials of ancient passenger stock run at weekends between Morpeth and Allendale, reversing in Platform 3 at Hexham.

Hexham is at ground level below the patio. The branch starts level at the side of the lawn, then rises near Allendale into the rockery. The main line to Scotsgap rises on two shelves (one above the other) bracketed to the left-hand fence. Scotsgap has three simple platforms (Up Main, Down Main and Reversing Loop), built on a stone causeway.

Front and side gardens: Ashington is a busy colliery town served by a triangular junction from the main line. Traffic is as follows:
- Coal trains run on to the main line at Bedlington, returning via the reversing loop R.
- Pick-up goods trains reverse and shunt in Ashington yard and bays.
- Freight tender engines can take coal and water in Ashington before reversing via the triangle of the (blue) main line.
- Morpeth-Hexham suburban passenger trains reverse in Platform 2, with the tank engine running round.
- Parcels vans can be left or picked up from the bays at both stations.
- Push-pull trains reverse in bay Platforms 1 or 3.

Both stations are at ground level. The line to Hexham descends gently on a natural slope while the line to Morpeth rises to waist level, first on an embankment and finally on a viaduct. On the approach to Morpeth, a single-track line on the right descends to whole-train overnight storage sidings beneath Morpeth.

Indoor section: Morpeth is a market town with a major railway junction (NER and NBR). Principal traffic is as follows:
- Expresses on the East Coast Main Line – see pages 62 and 63 for photographs.
- Main line trains depart from Platform 1 southwards, returning in due course via the

No. 15 Northumbria Garden Railway (continued)

BEDLINGTON

TO HEXHAM

TO MORPETH

COLLIERY

COAL

3 2 1

OVERALL ROOF

ASHINGTON

[Not to scale]

reversing loop R. The loco then runs across to the MPD for turning and servicing.

- Main line stock is periodically exchanged in the carriage sidings.
- Hexham suburban trains terminate in Platforms 4 and 5.
- Ashington push-pull trains terminate in Platform 6.
- Shunting in the local goods yard.
- Marshalling of pick-up goods trains which depart clockwise to all stations and return in due course via the reversing loop R.
- Full MPD activities for coaling, watering, turning and storage.

Operation: At Morpeth, operation and viewing are from either side of the baseboard, with duck-under access to the far side. There are normally two local operators at Morpeth, together with about six outside operators around the garden. The timetable is regulated by the Traffic Master who is located in the corner of the shed and who has headphone communication with all stations.

Construction: The site measures 48m by 22m, and the shed is 12m by 6m. An O gauge model railway project of this size would need to be undertaken by a club, charity or business, taking some ten years to complete. It would start with conversion of the cowshed, to include the following features:

- A new outer skin of Cotswold stone, together with a new roof, door, windows and insulation.
- An electricity supply for power, lighting, heating and an intruder security system.
- Kitting out with tools, shelves, railwayana, chairs, a radio and a refreshment bar.

Gardening: The outdoor lines run mostly around the lawn, requiring strimming every few weeks. Access to the various lawns and

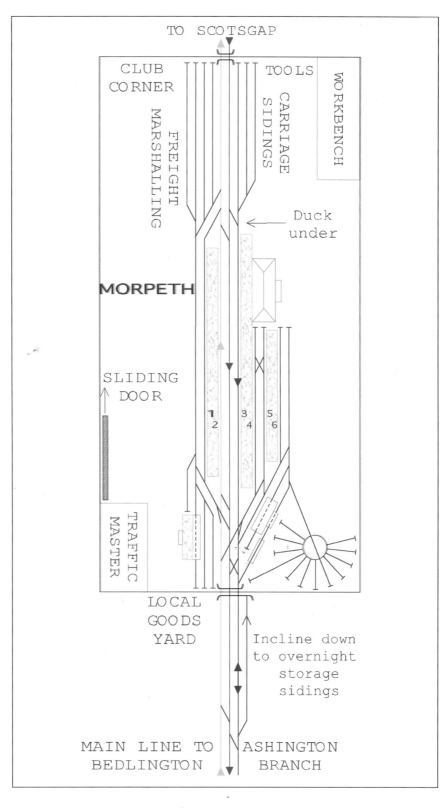

beds is by stepping over the main lines at lawn level. The elevated bed within the reversing loop through Scotsgap is planted with small shrubs while the rockery around Allendale is planted with

alpines suitable for 7mm scale (see photographs on page 98). The top section by the hedgerow is elevated on a viaduct and needs regular clearing of leaves, twigs and other debris.

In 1961, LNER A4 class Pacific No. 60029 Woodcock emerges from Stoke Tunnel near Grantham with the up 'Norseman' from Newcastle to King's Cross. Such a train would enhance Layout No.15. (Hugh Ballantyne)

In 1962, SR U class Mogul No. 31795 heads a pick-up goods train near Downton on the Salisbury to Bournemouth West line. Such a train would enhance Layout No. 16.

Above: Class W1 No. 10000 was an experimental 450psi water-tube boiler 4-6-4. In rebuilt form, resembling an A4 class, it is seen here in 7mm scale with the down 'West Riding Limited' on the Gainsborough Model Railway, about to take the bank up to Retford. Werrington Junction control panel is one of ten between King's Cross and Leeds. On operating nights, the building resounds with telegraph bells.

Right: Bridehaven is a fine example of a portable end-to-end layout suitable for exhibitions. Built by the Modern Image Group of the Weymouth Model Railway Association, it comprises a modest terminus with locomotive and freight yards, fed by a hidden fiddle yard. At the 2002 Spring Open Day, movement and interest were continual. Landscaping was well advanced, with buildings one of the next priorities. Built on three baseboards in OO gauge, it measures 5m by 0.8m overall.

16

A Shaftesbury Portable Layout

Summary description: An EM gauge portable end-to-end branch terminus with a fiddle yard.

Inspiration: The compact branch terminus is a classic configuration for those with meagre time, space or money to expend on modelling. Numerous examples can be seen at exhibitions and in magazines. Three of my favourites are Ken Payne's *Tyling Branch* (Ref. 35), the Leamington & Warwick Model Railway Society's *Walford* (Ref. 36) and Alan Parker's *Kettlewell*, (Ref. 37). The last-mentioned is modelled in N gauge and measures just 1.5m by 0.4m.

Geographical setting: Because of its strategic, elevated location (240m OD), Shaftesbury was bypassed by the LSWR West of England main line. The nearest station is two miles away at Semley, while Gillingham evolved as the main commercial centre of the area. As a result, Shaftesbury today is an historic market town, largely untouched by industry and epitomised in the Hovis advertisement where an old gent struggles up Gold Hill for his bread. My model aims to change all that with a new branch line which winds up the Nader Valley from a junction near Wardour Castle. Six miles long with an average gradient of 1 in 96, there are intermediate halts at Donhead St Andrew and Ludwell. The terminus at Shaftesbury then offers the perfect setting for my

kit-built BSL Bulleid coaches and goods wagons which are mentioned in Layout No. 6.

Design features:
- Although operated as a terminus, the station is modelled as a two-platform through-station, disappearing at the top end into a mirror under a road bridge.
- The station has a passenger bay and parcels bay.
- The station yard incorporates an engine shed and turntable.
- The running line disappears under a road bridge into the fiddle yard.
- The fiddle yard and goods yard are parallel, separated by a hillside of modest coverage so that fiddling and turning can be seen by spectators (on the left).
- The fiddle headshunt is hidden by an embankment.
- A novel, space-saving feature of the fiddle yard is the double-slip point on the turntable.

Control principles: One cab controller and a switching panel

are located by each turntable. The points and signals are manually operated using local levers, some of them ganged at the front of the baseboard. The turntables are handle-operated. Two point levers for the double-slip rotate with the turntable. Three-link and screw couplings are hand-operated using bent wire fixed to a torch.

Operation: Set in the late 1950s, regular services might comprise: pick-up goods trains; a push-pull shuttle service to Tisbury (LSWR gate stock); through trains to Salisbury (a three-coach LSWR corridor set) and through coaches to Waterloo (a four-coach Bulleid set). The last mentioned joins up at Salisbury with a similar set from Bournemouth West.

Construction: The four baseboards (having pink edges on the plan, with folding legs) bolt together, measuring 8.1m by 1.3m overall in EM gauge. Buildings, signals, scenery and accessories are modelled to fine-scale standards, as befits a small

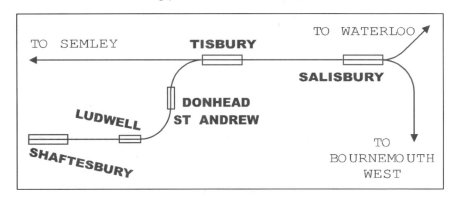

layout. An adventurous extension is to create a simple oval, with Tisbury modelled on the right-hand side as a junction station. One of the fiddle tracks then becomes a through-line and the main line oval dips down to pass to the left of Shaftesbury 'off-stage' at a slightly lower level. The Shaftesbury branch thereby becomes double-ended, running parallel with the LSWR main line.

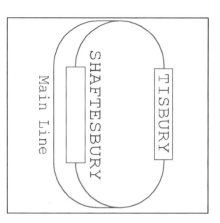

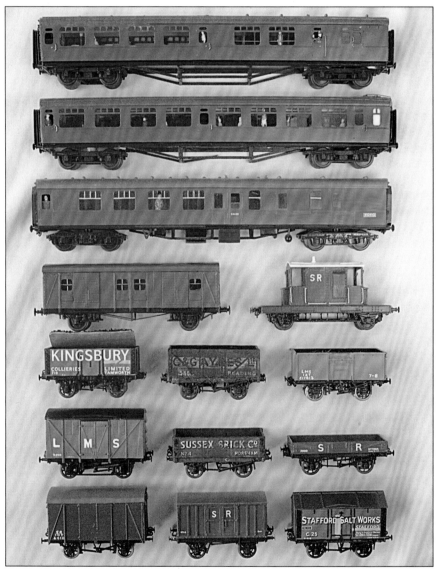

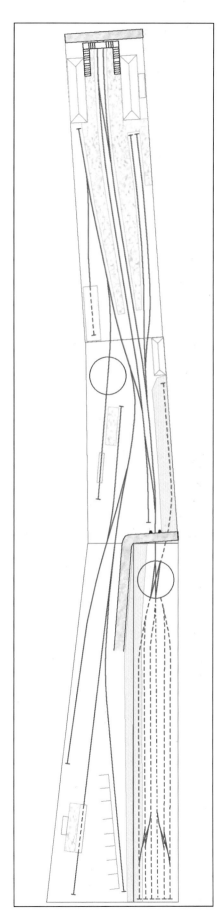

Some of my EM gauge kits: Rows 1 and 2: BSL Bulleid aluminium coaches with CCW bogies and Peco interiors. Row 3: Kitmaster BR(S) coach, plastic with a Peco interior kit. Row 4: Ratio SR 4-wheel utility van; and K's 25-ton brake van. Row 5: Peco seven-plank coal wagons (2); and an Airfix (plastic) steel mineral wagon. Row 6: Airfix meat wagon; Peco five-plank brick; and a Peco three-plank wagon. Row 7: Ratio SR van; K's SECR van; and a Peco Wonderful salt wagon. (Howard Warren).

17

Greater Paddington Garden Railway

Summary description: A double-track simple oval with a terminus, a through-station and a showpiece MPD.

Inspiration: The garden layout of the London Toy & Model Museum, Paddington, now sadly closed, as it was in the mid-1980s (below). Built in 2-rail O gauge, both stations were in full view as one descended the steps from the terrace to the viewing area along the side. The through-station had an inner loop platform for train reversals. Although the terminus had an MPD with a turntable, this was mainly for show since the railway could be operated in 'balanced' mode with tender locomotives facing either way, fifty-fifty. This balance and the need to disguise repetitive operations intrigued me.

Design features: After several trial designs, I rotated the terminus by 180° and put in a showpiece MPD at the top – shared by the two stations and having full ashing, coaling and turning facilities. I enlarged the through-station to two island platforms, using the outermost road for stopping trains, push-pull terminations and as a feeder to additional goods and industrial sidings along the left-hand, top and bottom sides. The original simple layout thereby became embellished with railway *divertissements* both inside and outside the oval, breaking the monotony of continuous running.

Control principles: Five wandering section controllers (Inner; Outer; Terminus; MPD; Goods Yard) connect to a lockable weather-proof control cubicle beneath Platforms 1 and 2. Points, uncouplers and the turntable are manually operated using rods, cranks and springs. Operators can stay in the well or one or two may transfer to the left-hand side for control of the goods sidings and the outer oval.

Operation: For public display, there might be one or two operating sessions daily (when dry). Just one trained staff member can run it, with two trains chasing their tails and the operator concentrating on a few locomotive movements and occasional whole train exchanges – passenger (inner oval) and freight (outer oval).

On club days, up to four operators and 'guest trains' provide greater variety and realism with more frequent reversals, proper shunting in the goods yard and full use of the MPD. Details of train reversals are then as follows:

- After a passenger train arrives in Platform 1, the loco runs forward to siding S and a fresh loco backs on to the rear from loop R. After train departure, the loco reverses into siding A for ashing, coaling and (partial) turning (about 90° anticlockwise). It then takes water, awaiting its next duty from the terminus.
- A departure from the terminus releases a loco to reversal loop R where it awaits its next duty in Platform 1 of the through-station. Care is needed to schedule the locos in the correct order.
- For a goods arrival in Platform 1, the loco runs forward via siding T to the coaling ramp, occasionally depositing or

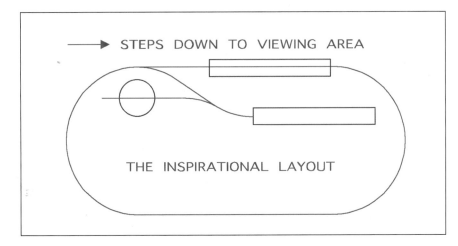

STEPS DOWN TO VIEWING AREA

THE INSPIRATIONAL LAYOUT

picking up a coal wagon. This allows the station pilot to add a brake van to the train from the end of siding T and to take the original brake van back to pilot siding P.

- When the goods train has departed with a fresh loco the first loco is free to enter siding A and the original brake van can be shunted to the end of siding T.
- After arrival in Platform 4 of the through-station, the goods engine runs forward while a shunter exchanges wagons in the goods yard or whole trains in the coal and oil sidings. Brake vans must also be exchanged. Meanwhile, the goods engine exchanges with another from the MPD, using the main line crossovers.
- Push-pull or DMU services add further variety, terminating in the bay of the terminus.

Construction: Depending upon the particular garden, visitors might be restricted to the left-hand side and the terrace (as at the museum), or there might be an all-round walkway. For five-coach trains in O gauge, the layout measures 7.1m by 3.2m. At least 1.5m must then be added to each spectator viewing side. The line needs to be about waist-high so that children can observe readily. A railed platform for toddlers is also a good idea. Operator access to the well is via a gate and steps from the terrace, creating a short railway tunnel. Such access then allows the entire railway to be laid on a solid foundation of a double skin of bricks filled with rubble, sand and cement – preferable to steel or wooden frames which will rot when exposed to the weather.

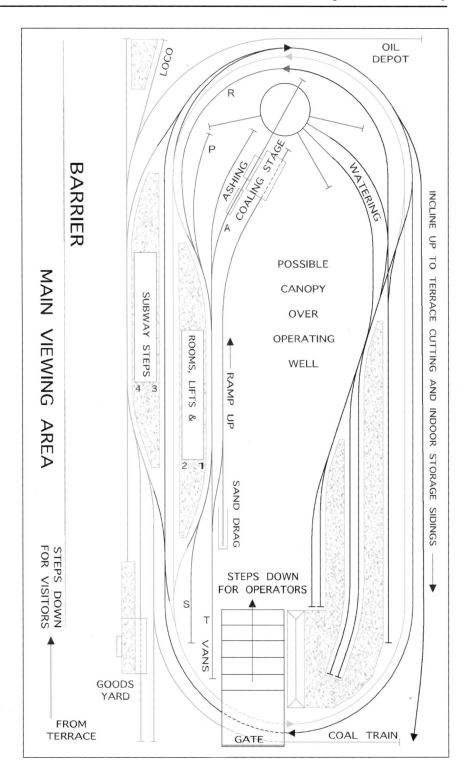

For secure storage, the incline on the right leads to a cutting at the right-hand end of the terrace and then to storage sidings suspended from the basement ceiling of the house.

18

Culverley & South Coast Club Layout

Summary description: A great spiralling OO gauge dumb bell on multiple levels throughout the upper storey of an Edwardian house. It represents LBSCR and LSWR stations from London to Brighton, Seaford and Portsmouth, with numerous branch lines and yards, with the emphasis upon operation.

Inspiration: A Peco OO gauge layout laid around two walls of my childhood bedroom in Culverley Road, Catford (corresponding to Guildford on the scale plan opposite). Forty years later, I extended the design to all the upstairs rooms, inspired by many whole-railway layouts, especially: Keith Ladbury's *GWR and LMS Lines* (Ref. 26); S. W. Stevens-Stratten's *South for Moonshine* (Ref. 38); Harry Fisher's *Cornwall & Devon* (Ref. 39); John Jay's *London, Bristol & South Wales* (Ref. 40); and the BR Brighton Staff Association's layout (Ref. 41).

Historical setting: The model can be set any time between the mid-1930s and the early 1960s – that golden era of the Southern Railway with an intriguing balance of steam and electric power (see photograph on page 72). The SR network was also interesting for having so many competing routes and junctions to the South Coast. The final touch is the London Underground, with the District and East London lines appearing from nowhere to terminate in SR suburban station bays.

Construction: A ten-year programme of construction, starting at the top levels and working down. Brightsea and Seaford have mid-point suspension from ceiling joists; elsewhere, wall brackets and floor posts are used. A perspex tunnel runs across the rear of the WC. An insulated timber box-tunnel bridges the external gap from Room 2 to the mess room, housing the double-track main

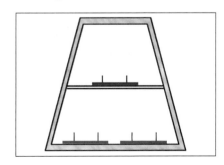

line with the single-track Hayling branch above.

For ease of access: all doors are removed; there is one step-over at floor level; several duck-unders at head-level; and platforms with steps are provided for observation of the uppermost stations. The mess room, store and workbench areas are important provisions for a club layout of this magnitude. Some 20 active members are envisaged, funded by a wealthy benefactor who lives on the ground floor.

Control principles:
- Section control, with segregation of operators for the up and down main lines.
- Additional operators for the branches and major yards.
- Brightsea, Fratton and Lewes are operated from a tall seat in Room 2, with a window to Room 1.
- Other control panels are local to stations and yards, wall-mounted where possible.
- Extensive use of bell codes, backed up by headphone sets.
- The Underground to run on auto (three trains to four termini) except when freight is passing through.

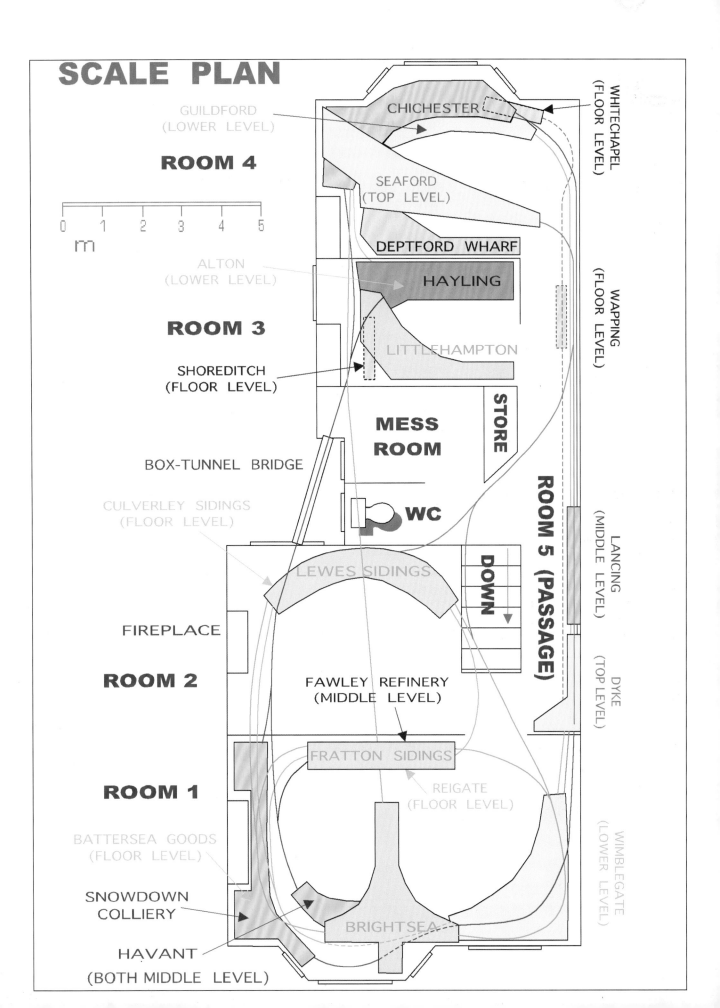

SCALE PLAN

ROOM 4

0 1 2 3 4 5
m

ROOM 3

GUILDFORD
(LOWER LEVEL)

CHICHESTER

WHITECHAPEL
(FLOOR LEVEL)

SEAFORD
(TOP LEVEL)

DEPTFORD WHARF

ALTON
(LOWER LEVEL)

HAYLING

WAPPING
(FLOOR LEVEL)

LITTLEHAMPTON

SHOREDITCH
(FLOOR LEVEL)

MESS ROOM

STORE

BOX-TUNNEL BRIDGE

CULVERLEY SIDINGS
(FLOOR LEVEL)

WC

LEWES SIDINGS

DOWN

ROOM 5 (PASSAGE)

LANCING
(MIDDLE LEVEL)

FIREPLACE

ROOM 2

FAWLEY REFINERY
(MIDDLE LEVEL)

DYKE
(TOP LEVEL)

FRATTON SIDINGS

ROOM 1

REIGATE
(FLOOR LEVEL)

BATTERSEA GOODS
(FLOOR LEVEL)

SNOWDOWN
COLLIERY

BRIGHTSEA

WIMBLEGATE
(LOWER LEVEL)

HAVANT
(BOTH MIDDLE LEVEL)

Operation: Generally one evening per week and one day per weekend. Various timetables according to the numbers of operators, to include any or all of the following services:

Express passenger steam:	Culverley	to Lewes
Local passenger steam:	Hayling	to Littlehampton or Seaford
Push-pull balloon + Terrier:	Brightsea	to Seaford and Dyke
Push-pull steam or 2-BIL (EMU):	Guildford	to Havant or Lancing or Chichester
Express EMU:	Reigate or Culverley	to Brightsea or Littlehampton
Suburban EMU:	Wimblegate	to Alton
Underground EMU:	Wimblegate	to Whitechapel or Shoreditch
Local freight:	Deptford	to Alton or Dyke
	Guildford	to Littlehampton or Seaford
Fitted freight:	Battersea	to Fratton
Parcels:	Brightsea	to Battersea or Culverley
Coal:	Snowdown	to Fratton
Fuel oil:	Fawley	to Fratton or Culverley

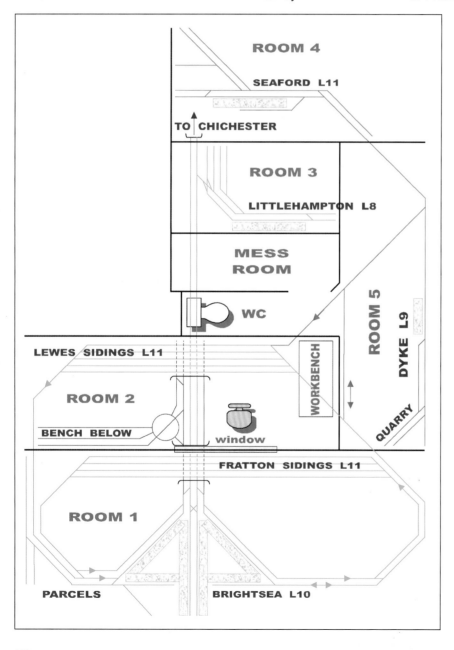

Accessories: Colour-light signalling for the main line, semaphores elsewhere, triggered by approaching trains and point positions. Robust rather than fine-scale modelling of the station buildings and yards. Rudimentary scenery with extensive use of backdrops. Modest up-lighting for the rooms and extensive use of spots and floods to focus upon the railway and its train services.

Schematic diagrams: Floor level is represented by L0 and head level is L10. To follow the main line, start at Culverley sidings (opposite page), follow the blue and red sections, then continue on the green section (this page) to Brightsea, Fratton or Lewes. A full circuit of the dumb bell measures 285m which is 13½ miles in 4mm scale. A non-stop train travelling at 50mph therefore takes about 16 minutes to complete a full circuit.

A goods train travelling from Deptford to Dyke (via Culverley and Seaford) takes up to an hour travelling at 25mph, or up to two hours if it stops at all stations for wagon exchanges and shunting. By contrast, single journeys by Underground or on the Hayling branch take just a couple of minutes.

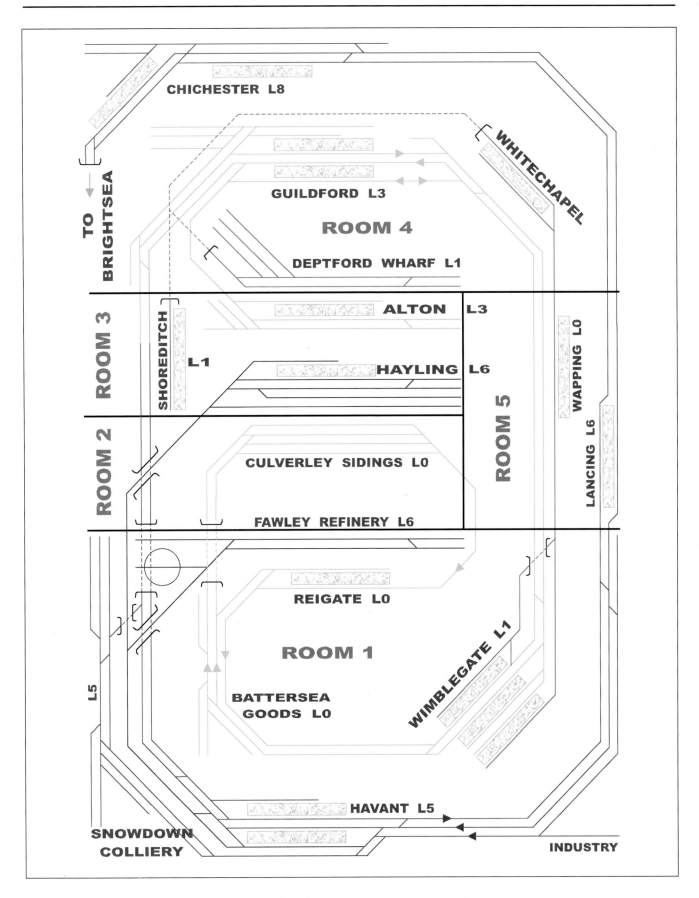

CHICHESTER L8

WHITECHAPEL

TO BRIGHTSEA

GUILDFORD L3

ROOM 4

DEPTFORD WHARF L1

ROOM 3

SHOREDITCH

L1

ALTON L3

HAYLING L6

WAPPING L0

ROOM 5

LANCING L6

ROOM 2

CULVERLEY SIDINGS L0

FAWLEY REFINERY L6

REIGATE L0

ROOM 1

WIMBLEGATE L1

L5

BATTERSEA GOODS L0

HAVANT L5

SNOWDOWN COLLIERY

INDUSTRY

Above: An inspiration for Layout No. 18 was the juxtaposition of steam and electric trains, on the Southern. Here at Swanley, a 'Schools' class 4-4-0 brings a train off the main line from Chatham, passing a suburban EMU in the siding. The photograph was taken in 1959 shortly before the change of up and down track designations from UUDD to UDUD.

Left: An inspiration for the Marine station of Layout No. 21 was the ferry facilities at Dover. Moored at the seaward end of Admiralty Pier is SS Shepperton Ferry, one of the Southern's coal-fired train ferries for the Dunkirk service. Built in 1936, it could accommodate 12 sleeping cars and some 40 goods wagons or up to 100 motorcars. Note the inlays of timber, paving bricks and tarmac between the rails.

Opposite: Two examples of simple oval by members of the Weymouth Model Railway Association.

Above: Phil Dawling's N gauge 'Filswey' has a bi-level storage yard and control panel hidden behind a scenic backdrop. The finger-loops above the panel are for the scratch-built signals at the GWR station. The station and scenery are finely detailed but to many visitors, the storage yard holds equal fascination. Built on two baseboards, it measures 1.2m by 0.8m.

Right: The 'Pen Mill' Group's OO gauge 'Yeovil Pen Mill' was operational in Spring 2002 but with scenery only partially completed. Depicting the inter-war years, a GWR train from Weymouth connects with an SR push-pull set. The line to Yeovil Town branches off (top right). General sidings are on the left. Operation is from the central well with storage loops along the left-hand side. An external operator controls the goods yard (bottom, out of shot) while the remaining sides (right and top) are for spectator viewing. Built in 12 sections, the layout measures 6.1m by 2.4m

19

Barnehurst Top Shed Railway

Summary description: An extensive double oval in O gauge, with a principal through-station and a long branch line, suitable for a large garden shed, basement or hall. Representative trains are envisaged from the Big Four railways of the 1923-48 era, featuring express passenger trains in particular.

Inspiration: The Smart family – parents and three sons – friends of our family who lived at Barnehurst, Kent, and indulged in many types of engineering. The eldest son built a yacht which he sailed to America. His father built a room over their garage-cum-workshop where they installed a model railway around the walls. Built in pre-war O gauge with outside-third rail pick-up, it was a double-track simple oval with a goods yard in one corner and a branch to a low-level terminus. Access to the central area was via a hinged bridge across the door (see diagram, right).

When I developed the design into a double oval, the lifting bridge became bi-level, the branch became long at high-level, the yard moved to low-level and a great through-station was added along the left-hand side. It was inspired also by the sheer spectacle of W. S. Norris's *Stroudley & Francisthwaite* (Ref. 42) – that finest of O gauge layouts – which was also built in a purpose-built garden shed. The choice of Allhallows-on-Sea for the terminus reflects the Southern's bold plan to promote holiday and commuter traffic.

Design features:
- A double-track main line with a long single-track branch to a high-level terminus.
- Two turntables, with over-generous locomotive storage at the terminus.
- Reversing platforms between the two halves of the through-station.
- A low-level goods loop, yard and halt, connected to the inner oval.
- Two hidden sidings connected to the outer oval.

Control principles: Digital control is suitable for running two trains on each of the main lines (red and blue) and for shunting at the stations and yards. All control positions could be in the central area, but if regular visitors are envisaged, it would be better to control most movements from outside the oval at the top and bottom ends, with just one or two operators inside the oval for fine control of shunting. Cab control is a good alternative.

Operation: There is continuous running of two trains per track around the double oval, with periodic exchanges to the terminus, goods loop, hidden sidings **E** and **F**, and reversing Platforms **3** and **4**. Passenger train reversals at Barnehurst avoid crossing any running line by the following procedure:
- After arrival in Platform **4**, the locomotive runs forward to siding **B**.
- The station pilot shunts the carriages into siding **C**, then returns to siding **A**.
- After turning at the MPD, the loco draws the train into Platform **3** ready for departure.

Freight train operation is a little different: after shunting in the lower yard, the loco runs round the Hoo loop, ready to return the train (clockwise) to the main line;

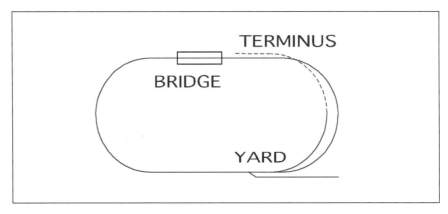

tender engines must then turn in Barnehurst MPD by running (tender-first) into Platform **3** and reversing the train into siding **D** before proceeding to the turntable.

Together with further locomotive movements and shunting at Allhallows-on-Sea, such detailed procedures are important for operator and visitor interest, breaking the uniformity of continuous running around the ovals. Push-pull services between Allhallows and Hoo Halt add further variety by 'filling in' between express and freight services.

Construction: Although the inspirational layout was around the walls of the shed, the greater width and multiple levels of this new development demand all-round access for construction, control and maintenance. The layout measures 12m by 5m in O gauge to which some half-metre must be added all round for access. Indeed, the top end could be extended further to become a workshop for locomotive servicing. The entire layout is supported on timber or Dexion floor columns, constructed bottom-up in phases over a period of some three to five years. If accommodated in a purpose-built shed, the best part of a year must be added for shed planning, construction and fitting out. To avoid sun glare, any windows should be north facing.

Accessories: Fine detail of architecture, furniture, vehicles and people at the stations and yards, together with landscaping of the cuttings and embankments

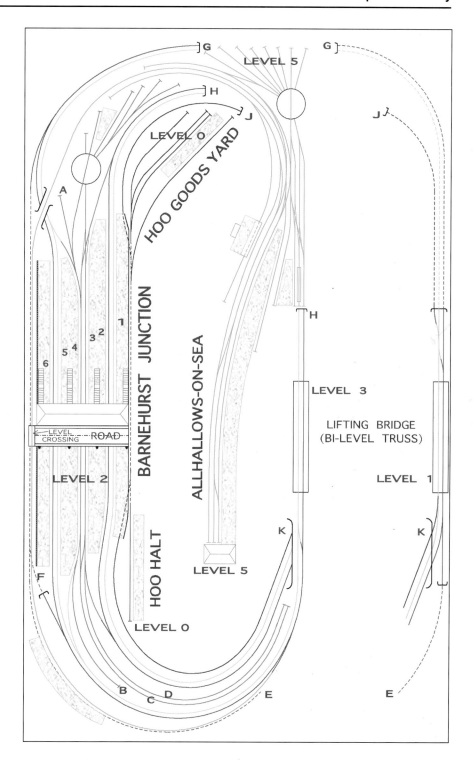

and some colourful backdrops on the walls. For a layout of this size, however, the greater effort is likely to be expended on the construction of locomotives and rolling stock.

20

The BR Memorial Line

Summary description: A double oval with a high-level terminus and a low-level through-station. It displays a variety of train types from the early years of BR. The emphasis is upon steam but with a few first-generation diesel locos and a DMU.

Inspiration: The BR Exhibition Layout – a scenic O gauge double oval – which 'did the rounds' around 1950, remembered as an 'impression' rather than for detail. I simply developed the stations and yards to make the static and shunting elements more interesting. The overall objective is to create a spectacle of continuous movement, with a variety of train types making surprise appearances.

Design features:
- A double-track main line with just three facing points and only one level crossing.
- A diagonal terminus on the upper level with a goods yard and a showpiece MPD.
- A truss bridge across one end of the through-station.
- An outer loop serving the lower goods yard, sector plate and coaling stage.
- Suitable for any gauge but especially suitable for exhibitions in OO.

The two stations have interesting pointwork and yards, contrasting with the blandness of the ten parallel tracks along the right-hand 'country' side. The merits of the design may be compared with Layout No. 19 also a double oval but with the bridge on the 'country' side and a double station. See diagram below.

Control principles: Digital control is a good choice for running two trains on each main line (up and down) and for movements in the yards and sidings. There are two control positions:
- The central well – for the main lines and terminus (two persons).
- The bottom left-hand corner – for the outer loop and lower yard (one or two operators).

Operation: The layout is intended for continuous running with two trains on each of the main lines (red and blue). These exchange systematically with a third train in Platform **1** (down) and Platform **3** (up). Whole trains also exchange with others from the storage sidings. In a curious quirk of geometry, trains must take the innermost Platform **1** (and the purple loop) in order reach the outermost Platform **4** (or the adjacent goods reception road). To reverse, the locomotive then runs forward to the sector plate and subsequently runs around the outer loop to the rear of the train. After return to the terminus, a station pilot draws the train forward for release of the locomotive via the crossover.

Construction: This is a portable exhibition layout, with a dedicated motor van for storage and transport. Measuring 4.6m by 2.5m in OO gauge, there are eight lower baseboards – four along each long side (with folding legs) plus two (legless) baseboards which bridge the top and bottom ends. Four upper baseboards (with legs) rest partly upon the lower baseboards. The truss bridge is added when all else is in place. At exhibitions, crowd barriers are installed about half a metre away on the three viewing sides (left, top and bottom). The standard of finish is robust rather than fine-scale, with plenty of people and platform furniture.

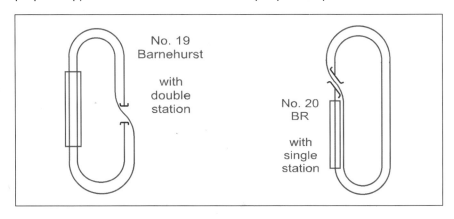

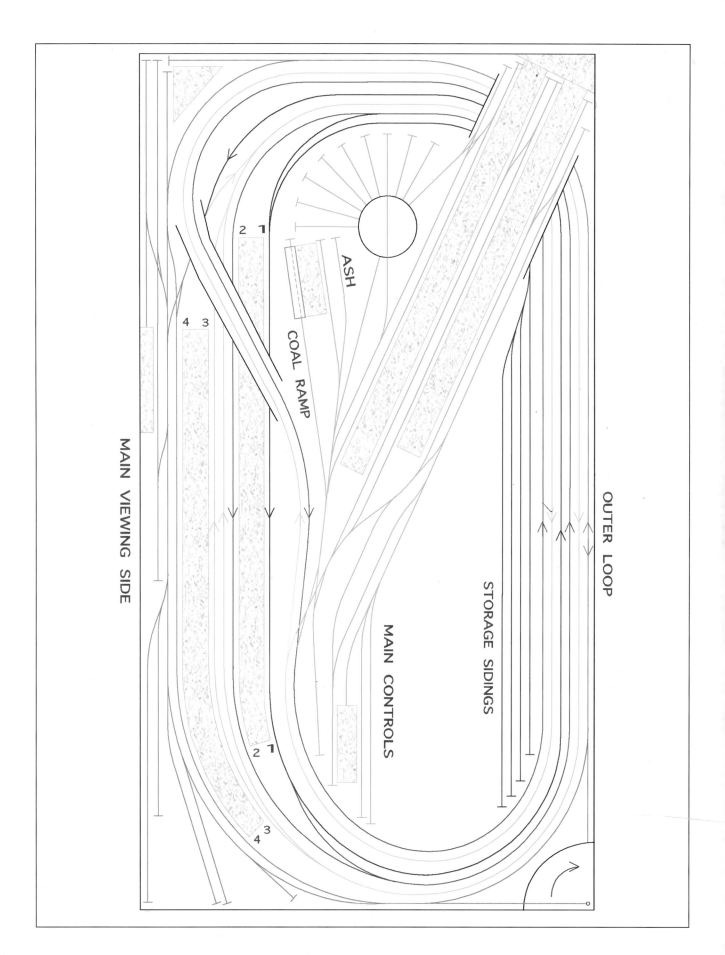

MAIN VIEWING SIDE

ASH

COAL RAMP

2 1

4 3

MAIN CONTROLS

2 1

4 3

STORAGE SIDINGS

OUTER LOOP

21

Mayfield & Saxonhaven Club Layout

Summary description: Reversing loop with an upper-level main line and a low-level port and colliery.

Inspiration: The *Maycroft Railway*

(Ref. 43) was a classic reversing loop in O gauge, as shown in this simplified diagram (right). At the Model Railway Club's 1959 Easter Exhibition at the Central

Hall, Westminster, I stood mesmerised for an hour as a succession of beautiful trains from the 1930s emerged from the carriage sidings to be taken on

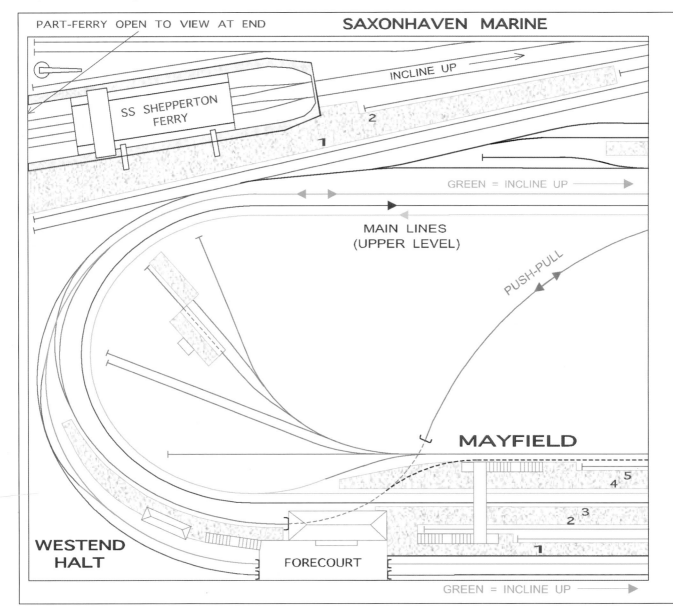

PART-FERRY OPEN TO VIEW AT END   SAXONHAVEN MARINE

INCLINE UP

SS SHEPPERTON FERRY

2

1

GREEN = INCLINE UP

MAIN LINES
(UPPER LEVEL)

PUSH-PULL

MAYFIELD

5
4

3
2

1

WESTEND
HALT

FORECOURT

GREEN = INCLINE UP

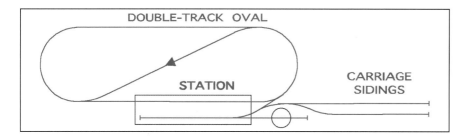

Double-track oval / Station / Carriage sidings

tours of duty, returning some 20 minutes later.

Design Features: By introducing low-level ovals with a major port and a colliery, the original railway is virtually doubled in size, making it a permanent club project rather than a portable exhibition line. The upper oval, through-station and MPD are similar to the original *Maycroft* but the carriage shed is turned 90° to act as a screen for the new low-level MPD and workshop. The reversing loop now passes beneath the double-track main line via two long inclines, plus a third incline (bottom) to make a new (green) undulating oval. Finally, I have added a general goods yard at Mayfield and seven short platforms for push-pull trains. The idea is to produce a stunning display of many types of train on different levels.

Control and operation: In full operation, four dedicated signalmen control switching panels located at Mayfield Inner, Mayfield MPD, Westend and Saxonhaven. Up to eight cab-

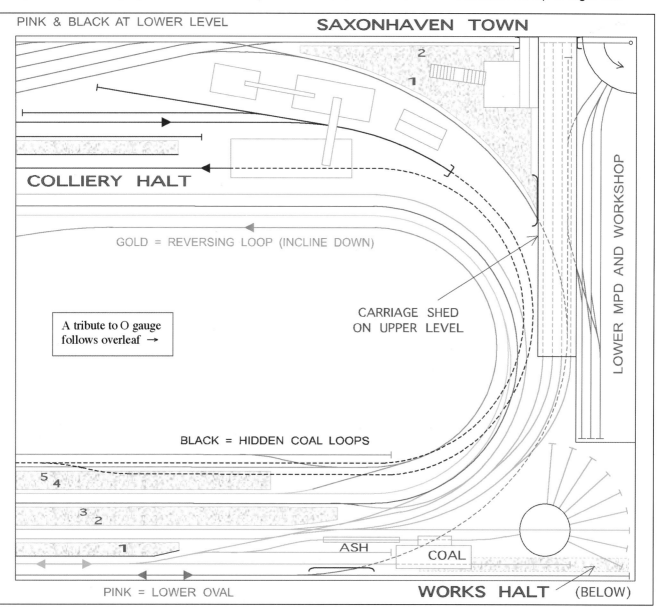

PINK & BLACK AT LOWER LEVEL

SAXONHAVEN TOWN

COLLIERY HALT

GOLD = REVERSING LOOP (INCLINE DOWN)

CARRIAGE SHED ON UPPER LEVEL

A tribute to O gauge follows overleaf →

BLACK = HIDDEN COAL LOOPS

LOWER MPD AND WORKSHOP

ASH

COAL

PINK = LOWER OVAL

WORKS HALT (BELOW)

enginemen then operate any or all of the following services:

- Boat trains between Mayfield and Saxonhaven include the 'Bronze Arrow' of Pullmans and the 'Nightwatchman' of *Wagons-lit*. They run via the main line and the reversing loop into Town station and then reverse either into Marine Platform 1 or on to the ferry.
- Other main line passenger trains operate out and back from Mayfield via the reversing loop.
- All main passenger and parcels trains rotate in sequence from the carriage shed via Mayfield.
- Three push-pull sets shuttle in sequence between Mayfield Platform 1, Works Halt, Colliery Halt, Marine Platform 2, Town Platform 2 and Mayfield Platform 5 (always avoiding the main lines).
- A Continental freight operates out and back from Saxonhaven ferry, reversing in Town.
- General freight trains operate between Marine quay sidings and Mayfield goods yard.
- Coal trains - one full and one empty – take turns on the upper and lower ovals via the colliery.
- Both MPDs are kept busy with locomotive turning and servicing.

Construction: Designed for O gauge, the layout measures 10.6m by 5.5m plus at least 1m all round for access, operation and visitors. This is a major club project with a construction programme of at least ten years. Conventional baseboards comprise Sundeala on a deal frame with timber support posts. The greatest effort is concentrated on the fine-scale trains, trackwork, buildings and scenery.

Inspirations for Saxonhaven:
- Channel ports inspired the twin stations, especially Harwich, Newhaven, Dover and Folkestone.
- The Bury St Edmunds Model Railway Club's evocative *Abbotsford* (Ref. 44) inspired the Marine platform (though their Marine station was later changed into carriage sidings).
- John Allen inspired the train ferry (Ref. 22) - his ferry could even move across synthetic water.
- J. R. Wall's *Hebdon Junction* (Ref. 45) inspired modelling just the platform ends at Town station.
- Frank Dyer's compact *Borchester Town* (Ref. 46) inspired the colliery where he had full and empty trains appearing and disappearing in opposite directions via hidden storage loops.
- The low-level MPD with sector plate is my own idea.

A tribute to O gauge: Until about 1950, more layouts existed in O gauge than in any other scale. Standards ranged from very coarse

Gainsborough (Ref. 53) is currently the largest O gauge model railway in British outline, depicting the East Coast Main Line between London and Leeds. It is built in an old school measuring 17m by 17.5m overall. Construction started in the Leeds room in 1949 (see photograph, opposite) but spread to the King's Cross room (above) and to the corridor behind the camera. There are nine stations, three goods yards, five MPDs with turntables and 365m of main line (12 scale miles). Featured in this picture (left to right) are: the main line loop; the Retford bank; Hornsey station; and Gasworks Tunnel through to King's Cross (far left) whose signalman has his back to the camera. All the signals are working – the semaphores in the foreground are the Retford down homes. A further photograph of this breathtaking railway is on page 63.

to fine, with propulsion by clockwork, outside-third, centre-third, stud-contact, two-rail and live steam. Live steam is now rare in O gauge, but articles in *Model Railway News* (Ref. 47) show that it is practical. The magic of O gauge derives from size, a long train being capable of enthralling the viewer, even on fairly simple layouts. In addition to *Maycroft* (Ref. 43), some of my indoor favourites are:

- The *Sherwood Section of the LMSR* (Ref. 48). Probably the best clockwork layout, it was designed for intensive operation, bristling with junctions, stations and locomotives.
- *Stroudley & Francisthwaite* (Ref. 42). One of the finest electric layouts, it was designed for pre-Grouping realism and taking up to 15 minutes to complete one circuit. Sadly, the owner died before completion.
- *Bromford & High Peak* (Ref. 49). This inherited much of the trackwork from *Stroudley & Francisthwaite*. It features some stunning scenery in a maze of ovals, loops and sidings.
- *Kirtley*, at the Derby Industrial Museum, is a magnificent tribute to the Midland Railway (see photograph, page 82).
- The West Lancashire O Gauge Group layout features a four-track oval with flying junctions to a terminus (Ref. 50).
- *Pacific Seaboard Lines* is a huge complex of multiple ovals set in New South Wales (Ref. 51).
- *Wallsea Main* (Ref. 30). One of the best exhibition layouts, it is a simple oval with storage sidings on one side and a stunning, highly detailed station on the other. Long trains are a speciality.
- *Abingdon* (Ref. 52) is a one-man, fine-scale branch terminus seen at the 2001 National Exhibition.

On the 'Gainsborough' model railway, over 110 locomotives and some 350 items of rolling stock are mostly scratch-built to fine-scale O gauge. Points are hand-built and track is manufactured by Peco. Operators control points and trains in their respective electrical sections. Leeds Central signalman, control panel and MPD are seen here in the foreground on an operating night (Mondays). The other three signalmen (left to right) are at Hitchin, Decoy Goods and Doncaster. In 2002, construction work (on Thursday nights) was concentrating on scenery and buildings including the completion of the overall roof at Leeds Central (left). The society has about 30 members and is a member of the Lincolnshire Museums Forum. Open weekends can attract up to 1,000 visitors – a tiring, all-day experience for the signalmen.

Two fine-scale O gauge model railways called 'Kirtley' have been built as a tribute to the Midland Railway. Don Neal's garden line was one (Ref. 33). The other was completed in 1951 by Derby Museum & Art Gallery and in 1982, it was decided to rebuild it in the Derby Industrial Museum. It comprises a simple oval with a junction station on one side and storage sidings behind a ceiling-high backdrop. On the public side, a glazed partition, 16m long, gives uninterrupted views down the long reverse sweep of the station, with lighting from fluorescent boxes angled at 45°. Using in-house project management, it was built by a mix of contractors, museum staff and volunteers. Reconstruction in its present form started in 1992 and the trackwork was completed in 2002 using a temporary control system for operation for the public once a month. Outstanding work includes coin-in-the-slot automation, completion of buildings and scenery, signalling and a computerized control system. From historical research to wiring, the work throughout is to a high standard. The track adheres closely to Midland practice, built by contractor Norman Solomon. At the far end of the photograph, scenic work is in progress around Kirtley station building while in the foreground, two trains are stabled in the goods yard. Locomotives and rolling stock are a mix of originals from the 1950s and '60s, new kits, scratch-building and second-hand acquisitions. In the picture, Johnson 0-4-4 tank No. 1278 (bottom right) was built by the late Ross Pochin of the Manchester Model Railway Society, possibly started in the 1930s in coarse-scale. Alongside, Kirtley 0-6-0 No. 753 is another early model, built by John Keenan in 1951 and rebuilt by David Moore in 1997. The ammonia tank wagon (between the locos) was built by Paul Doggett in 1994. The dining carriage (left) is one of an award-winning pair built in 1955 by the late Charles M. Shoults, again of the MMRS.

22

Holborn & Crystal Palace Club Layout

Summary description: A simple oval with long sides separated by the Crystal Palace of the 1920s.

Inspiration: Following the publication of my book *The Last Days of Steam on the Southern; SECR*, I received an enquiry from the Norwood Model Railway Club for photographs of the short-lived LCDR Blackfriars Bridge station (which closed in 1885). Their 4mm scale model can be previewed on www.hhwcomputing.demon.co.uk /norwoodmrc. I was further inspired by two books in the London Suburban Railways series by the Middleton Press, respectively from Holborn Viaduct and to Crystal Palace High Level. My idea is to combine these two

stations (plus Ludgate Hill) into a single model railway, set in the late 1920s with a mix of steam and electric services.

Historical setting: Due to piecemeal development, the LCDR had too many commuting stations in the City of London. All four were in use together from 1874 to 1916 (see diagram, below). There was also passenger and freight through-traffic to the Widened Lines at Farringdon (see

Layout No. 4). It was an area busy with short ancient trains. Standards for passengers improved following electrification to Holborn Viaduct in 1925 but the stations remained cramped and primitive compared with other surface stations in the City. When the through line was rebuilt in 1990, Holborn Viaduct closed and a new through-station opened as St Paul's Thameslink.

The Crystal Palace High Level branch opened in 1865 to serve

Ludgate Hill originally had two island platforms and an overall roof. It was remodelled during 1907-12 to create just one island platform – wider and with a canopy. In 1959, 30 years after closure, it was photographed from the south. The 4-SUB unit is en route to Holborn Viaduct. The walls of the former overall roof are visible on either side. The lattice signal post has an LCDR finial and carries SR colour-lights. The visitors are students in railway history from Goldsmiths College.

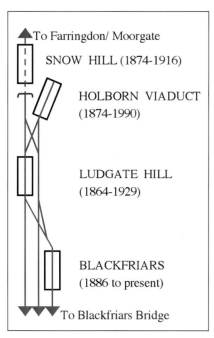

To Farringdon/ Moorgate

SNOW HILL (1874-1916)

HOLBORN VIADUCT (1874-1990)

LUDGATE HILL (1864-1929)

BLACKFRIARS (1886 to present)

To Blackfriars Bridge

the Great Exhibition. The terminus was a fine piece of architecture, complementing the grandeur of the exhibition. The line was electrified in 1925 but the exhibition burnt down in 1936, traffic declined and the branch closed in 1954. Sidings at Crystal Palace were used partly for goods but also for storage of old steam stock.

Design features:
- The layout has two long sides separated by a tall partition.
- The Crystal Palace exhibition building is modelled in low relief on one side of the partition.
- Between the palace and the railway, the Parade is adorned with buses, trees and people.
- The City of London skyline is painted on the other side of the partition, including the Old Bailey and St Paul's Cathedral, with an in-fill of roof-tops.
- The hidden end-loops complete a simple oval between Crystal Palace and Ludgate Hill.
- There is all-round access, with

the tunnels and end-loops open to view at either end.
- Crystal Palace station is at low level, with just the platform ends visible beneath the roof. The hidden terminal tracks then dip and curve sharply below Holborn Viaduct.
- Only the ends of the platforms and roof are modelled at Blackfriars. A plastic strip curtain covers the four unelectrified tracks as they enter the bridge across the Thames.
- Two of the tracks across the bridge (gold) represent Eardley carriage sidings, with a traverser for locomotive run-round. A Victorian mansion is modelled above the traverser.
- Modest locomotive storage is provided by the loops at either end. Others are stored on shelves below the baseboard.
- Station layouts represent the late 1920s but with some modification of pointwork. Purists would demand more

precise configurations, requiring more space.
- One major omission is the Crystal Palace turntable which connected all four terminal tracks at the left-hand end. Locomotives are 'turned' instead by balanced operation.
- The most adventurous of clubs might include not only the turntable but moving traffic along the Parade with a roundabout at either end, using a proprietary magnetic roadway system. This increases baseboard length by half a metre to the left, allowing the front of Holborn Viaduct station to be modelled.

Construction: As drawn, the layout measures 11.0m by 2.5m overall in 4mm scale, to which at least one metre must be added all round for access, operation and viewing. Intended as a permanent club project, construction comprises conventional Sundeala board laid upon a framework of

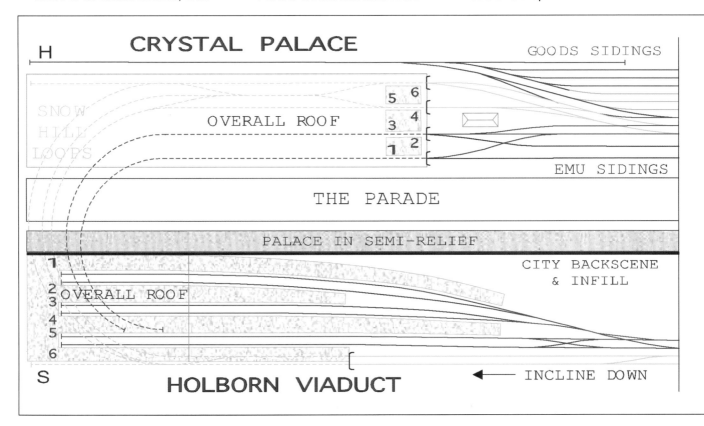

deal with timber support columns. The partition and the palace frontage can be built and painted off-stage in sections. Fine-scale modelling of buildings is appropriate but the tight end-curves call for OO rather than P4. Construction would take some five to ten years.

Control principles: Cab control is envisaged, with two signalmen in charge of mimic switching panels at the ends. Up to eight cab-drivers are then located around the layout.

Operation: For simple public demonstrations, EMUs run end to end between Crystal Palace and Holborn Viaduct while steam passenger, freight and parcels trains trundle round the (blue) oval. On club nights teams indulge in more authentic operation to include any of the following services from the 1920s:

- EMUs run between Holborn Viaduct (Platforms **1**, **4** and **5**)

and Crystal Palace (Platforms **1** and **2**).

- Parcels trains run between Holborn (Platforms **2**, **3** and **6**) and Eardley sidings.
- Empty Thanet stock works up from Eardley sidings into Ludgate Hill and back to Cannon Street, with the main line tender loco running round. This practice did not start until after Ludgate Hill had closed, but it adds interest here.
- Local steam passenger trains run between Snow Hill and Crystal Palace (Platform **5**).
- Goods trains run between Snow Hill and Crystal Palace, using 'balanced operation' to simulate use of the Palace turntable as follows:

A goods train arriving at the Palace runs directly into the headshunt **H**. After shunting in the yard, the loco draws the wagons from the tailshunt **T** into Platform **6** and uncouples. In the case of a tank engine, it simply runs round

and departs with the train, doing likewise at Snow Hill. A tender engine, on the other hand, runs forward from Platform **6** and reverses into siding **S**. An identical tender engine (facing the other way) then runs out of Platform **5** at the Palace and reverses on to the train. Upon arrival at Snow Hill, the two tender locomotives again exchange, also transferring a brake van to the rear.

Note that Snow Hill and Eardley Sidings are on inclines, requiring a brake bar to be inserted between the wheels of a stationary train.

Locomotives and rolling stock:

- Early SR EMUs arranged as 3-car motor units and 2-car trailer units.
- Thanet passenger trains - one of SECR 'birdcage' stock and one of early Maunsells.
- Local condensing trains include 6-wheel coaches from the LCDR, GNR and MR.
- Goods engines are condensing tanks and 0-6-0s.

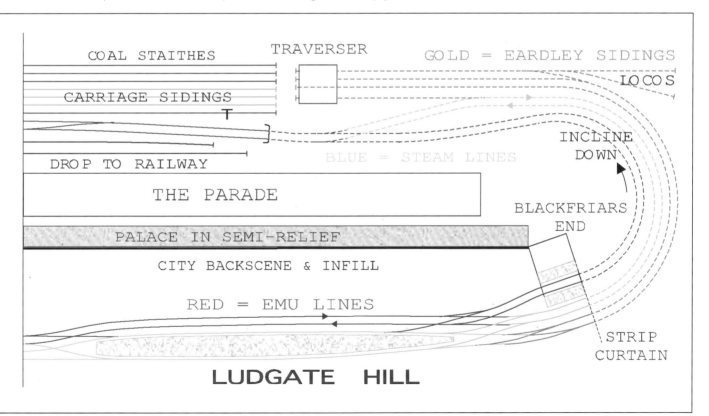

LUDGATE HILL

23

The Ultimate Hornby Dublo Layout

Summary description: A flat figure of eight with a terminus, two goods depots and a through-station on the reversing loop, intended for intensive operation using 3-rail Hornby Dublo or modern equivalent.

Inspiration: An article in *Railway Modeller* (Ref. 54) by Ian Hamilton describing his large Hornby Dublo layout which was built in a room over his garage. It is a simple oval with a triangular junction to a central terminus (see simplified diagram, right). I admired the long continuous run, the impressive terminus, the abundance of sidings and the discrete MPD. My development is to combine the two stations with an extra junction at the top, and to create a second goods depot by moving the MPD inside the oval (logically next to the terminus). The most important

features are retained – to give the impression of a table-top railway laid out in an ordinary room of the house – and to be large enough to display virtually every Hornby Dublo locomotive, train variation and accessory from the golden years of 1938 to 1964. The title 'ultimate' is, of course, no more than a challenge.

Design features:
- A long double-track main line oval, suitable for two trains per track.
- A bi-directional reversing loop with a through-station, creating two inner ovals.
- A terminus and MPD alongside the through-station, with entry to carriage sidings.
- A goods loop and inner goods depot within the left-hand oval.
- An outer goods depot in one

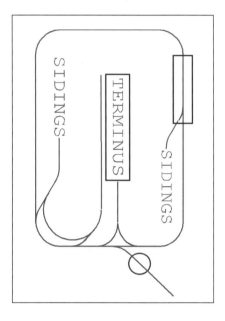

corner, using a fan of right-hand points.

Control principles: Seven section controllers are located as follows:

Terminus	light blue	- locally with manual points and uncouplers
Goods loop	gold	- locally with manual points and uncouplers
Inner goods depot	black	- locally with manual points and uncouplers
Outer goods depot	pink	- on main control panel with manual points and uncouplers
Outer oval	dark blue	- located on main control panel
Inner red oval	red	- located on main control panel
Inner green oval	green	- located on main control panel

The bi-directional reversing line (purple) has a three-position selector switch for dark blue/off/red.

For operation by just three or four people, an attractive option is for all points on the main line and reversing loop to be operated remotely from the main control panel. The cheaper alternative is to use manual points predominantly, with a pointsman at location P and just two points electrically operated (e). This would keep a team of six operators busy for operating sessions of about half an hour before becoming exhausted. Full operation is best described as 'hairy'.

Operation: The passenger terminus can be operated realistically by reversing every train into the sidings and turning the locomotive in the MPD. Alternatively, the carriage sidings can be operated like a second terminus with some arrivals routed via black-gold-purple and with every train reversing into or out of the real terminus so that locomotives need never uncouple. The MPD then becomes mainly a showpiece.

Goods services run between the two depots via the main lines. The inner goods depot has a small engine shed but no turntable, since trains can arrive and depart in either direction for 'balanced' operation. The goods loop is used for goods train reversals as well as for continuous running. EMU services also use the goods loop for services from the terminus to the gold bay, but they can depart the bay directly to the green oval.

Construction: The room measures 3.7m by 2.4m. Ian Hamilton used attractive kitchen base units (for household storage) along the left- and right-hand walls, topped with half-inch chipboard. The top and bottom of the layout were chipboard with support posts while the terminus was chipboard on a metal angle-frame. I cannot improve on that. For this adventurous layout, however, wide access is essential for the duck-unders to the inner operating wells.

Accessories: The layout is suitable for standard Hornby Dublo accessories including stations, turntable, signalboxes and signals. There is space for a few Dinky Toys in front of the terminus and in the two goods depots.

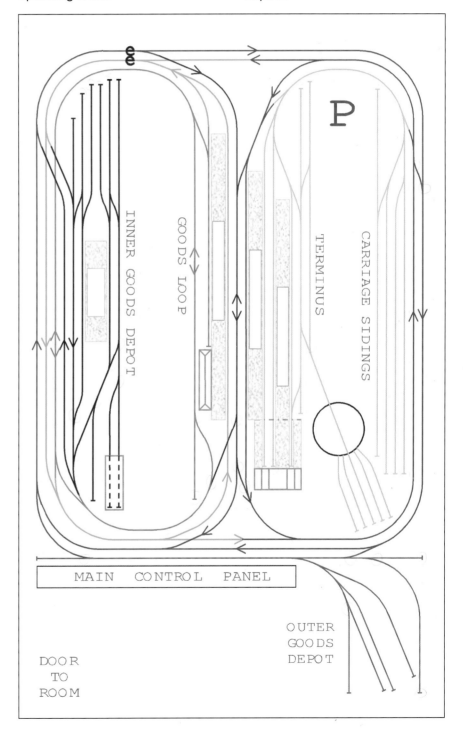

At the 2002 Mendip Exhibition, Donald and Gloria Hillyar display their Hornby Dublo landscaped layout 'Binns Road Junction' - a simple oval with reversing crossovers. Modelled as a tribute to Frank Hornby and his modelling industry, the Meccano factory siding is at the far end. The branch line rises to the foreground village of Maghull where he lived until his death in 1936. The buildings are mostly Hornby or Airfix. All rolling stock is pre-1952 and the locomotive motors are originals, never remagnetised.

24

Reading Stations Club Layout

Summary description: The GWR main line in a flat figure of eight; a GWR branch at high level; and an out-and-back SR cross-country loop at low level.

Inspiration: The actual Reading stations around 1960 - that intriguing juxtaposition of a grand high-level Great Western through-station with steam and diesel locomotives, alongside the more humble low-level Southern terminus - part steam and part electric – together with interconnecting spurs. The idea of a flat figure of eight came from Layout No. 23.

Design features:
- The GWR main and relief lines display a succession of long-distance trains.
- Reading General is modelled to show only the London end.
- Whole trains can be held in the Western cut-off sidings and on the freight loops.
- The SER line provides a variety of train types and EMUs.
- The GWR branch to Wallingford has freight and auto-trains.
- Passenger and freight trains can transfer between the GWR and SER systems.

Operation:
- A succession of trains from the Western cut-off sidings runs clockwise on the outer oval.
- A succession of freight trains trundles anticlockwise around the (blue) freight oval.

- One train runs anticlockwise on the up relief oval via Platform 6.
- Two trains cross in a flat figure of eight through Reading General via the down relief and down Newbury lines.
- From Reading South, steam trains run out and back around the SER loop and EMUs terminate at Reigate.
- Transfer trains are held in Reading General Platform 1 (from the SER) and in Platform 2 (to the SER).
- A typical sequence of GWR-SER train transfers is: Platform 2 to the SER; outer oval to Platform 2; up relief to the outer oval; figure of eight to the up relief; Platform 1 to the figure of eight; SER to Platform 1.
- Transfers also occur with the freight loop and Wallingford, using Platforms 3-4 for auto-trains or DMUs.

Geographical background: The long SER cross-country line from Redhill to Reading was built primarily as a strategic link to connect the Kentish Channel

ports directly with the LSWR at Guildford, the Army camps around Aldershot and with the GWR at Reading. The line was used also for outer suburban traffic as follows:
- SER trains from Reading to London Bridge via Guildford and Redhill (69 miles).
- LSWR trains from Reading to Waterloo via Ascot (43 miles, electrified in 1939).
- EMU services from Reigate to Redhill and London Bridge (electrified in 1932).

By contrast, the GWR main line into Paddington is just 36 miles and with non-stop fast trains. Various inclined spurs have connected Reading General to the SER, carrying through-traffic.

Control principles:
- Using cab control, a GWR master signalman is located at the left-hand side.
- Four GWR cab drivers are located on the left-hand side.
- Two SER cab drivers sit alongside Reading South.
- One SER cab driver sits

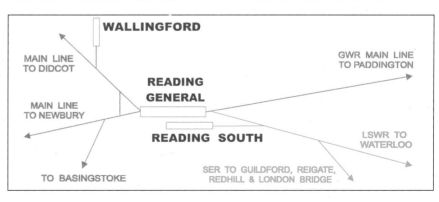

89

alongside Reigate.
- Bell codes are used for GWR/SER communication.
- Semaphore signal operation is triggered by approaching trains and point positions.

Construction: This major project requires a permanent clubroom. The layout itself measures 13m by 7.5m to which at least 1m must be added to the left-hand side for operators and viewing. The other three sides butt against the walls

of the clubroom, with baseboards supported on a combination of brackets, posts and storage cabinets. The left-hand and centre baseboards have support posts with carpeted crawl-through access tunnels to the two inner

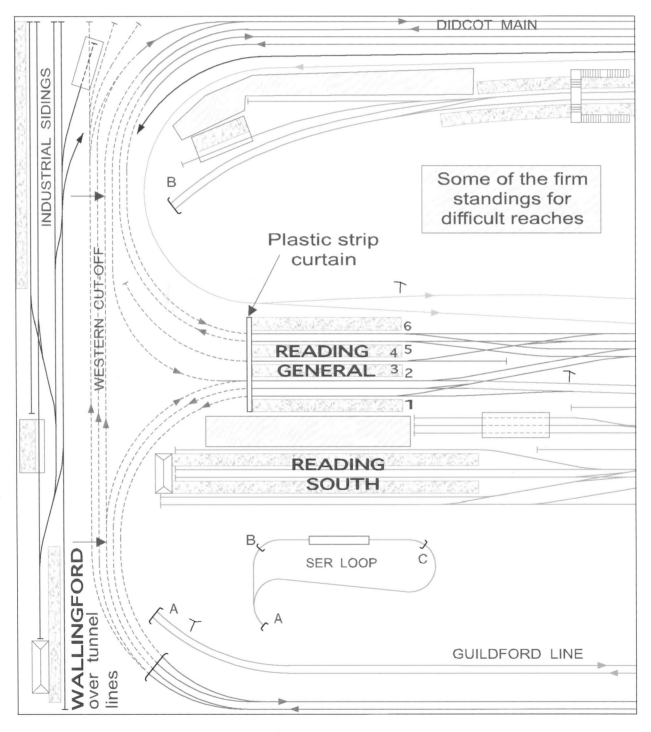

DIDCOT MAIN

INDUSTRIAL SIDINGS

WESTERN CUT-OFF

B

Some of the firm standings for difficult reaches

Plastic strip curtain

6
READING 4 5
GENERAL 3 2
1

READING SOUTH

B
SER LOOP
C
A
A

WALLINGFORD over tunnel lines

GUILDFORD LINE

wells. There are four levels of track – Wallingford (top) – GWR – Reading South – and Reigate (bottom). Some of the baseboards are too wide for normal reach, notably at Reading (2.4m reach), Reigate (1.9m reach) and at the

Eastern cut-off. Firm standings are therefore built into the baseboards for attention to trackwork, scenery or trains. Removable scenery covers these standings. There are backdrops and embankment scenery on the

three 'walled' sides while Reading and Wallingford rely mainly upon station features to set the trains off. There is enough construction work here to keep a club of ten active members busy for a decade or more.

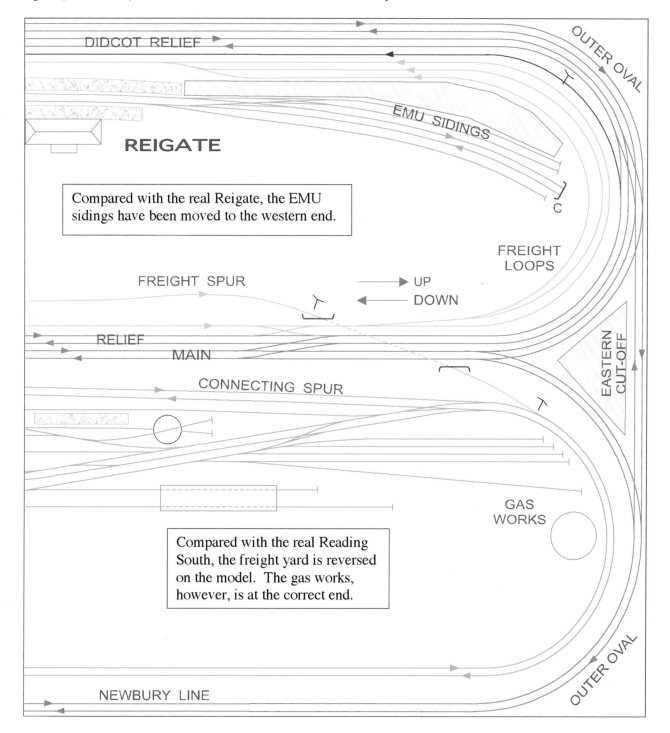

REIGATE

Compared with the real Reigate, the EMU sidings have been moved to the western end.

Compared with the real Reading South, the freight yard is reversed on the model. The gas works, however, is at the correct end.

25

The Huddersfield Loop Line

Summary description: An OO gauge figure of eight in an Edwardian L-shape attic bedroom.

Inspiration and setting: My student lodgings in Streatham had several L-shape rooms which lent themselves to figure-of-eight model railways. The dining room inspired Layout No. 2, *The Highland Garden Railway*, while my study-bedroom (narrower with equal arms) inspired this one. The figure of eight is the least common of the basic configurations. The best example that I have come across is *Beammas Junction*, built by the Huddersfield Railway Modellers (Ref. 55). They wanted their rejuvenated club layout to be viewed from all sides, with the storage yard hidden but accessible. The brilliant solution was a figure of eight, using one long diagonal for the storage yard and with a tight S-bend below. Both crossings are within the operating well but hidden by backdrops, as illustrated in the simplified layout plan (right). It was beautifully finished in OO gauge fine-scale. In honour of their achievements, I have set my own humble plan south of Huddersfield on the Lancashire & Yorkshire Railway.

Design features:
- A double-track main line in a figure of eight.
- A high-level terminus with a large goods yard and a modest MPD.
- A low-level through-station and a reversing loop **R**.
- Three small low-level goods yards.

Control principles: One elongated control panel alongside Holmfirth incorporates four cab controllers: Up Main; Down Main; Terminus A and Terminus B. Operation of points and uncouplers is manual except for the Brockholes sidings, one remote point on the reversing loop and one in the tunnel. There is scope for full semaphore signalling – probably wire-in-rod at the terminus but automatic motor-operated on the main line, triggered by approaching trains and point positions. The central control panel allows the entire railway to be operated by one person or by a group of up to four.

Operation: Main line passenger and freight trains take turns out and back from Holmfirth. There is normally one up and one down train running, with others held on the reversing loop **R** and in an up loop (**E** or **F**). Main line trains stop periodically at Brockholes, allowing a push-pull train to shuttle between the bays at Holmfirth and Brockholes. The daily pick-up goods train runs from Holmfirth via the three local, low-level yards.

The model has only modest provision for locomotive and

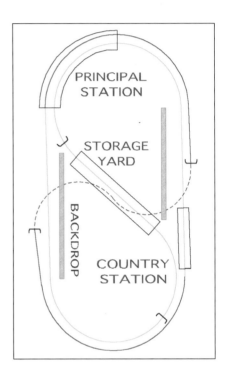

whole-train storage. To hold all those spare locomotives and rolling stock, a tall storage cabinet is therefore provided in the recess by the doorway. One shelf of this cabinet could be used for an extension of the railway into the second attic room across the landing, as outlined with Layout No. 26. Platform 1 and the freight headshunt then become through lines, handling much increased traffic. A new identity is then needed for Holmfirth, becoming an industrial port town on the Humber.

Historical theme: A photograph on page 99 shows Brockholes station building in 2002. The real Holmfirth branch closed in 1965 but the Keighley & Worth Valley Railway operates preserved steam services some 15 miles away to the north. An interesting option is to make the model a preserved line, allowing a wider variety of trains. Since the terminus is in *Last of the Summer Wine* country, locomotives can be named after Compo, Foggy and Clegg, with a restored Pullman car named *Nora Batty* and with wrinkly stockings on sale in the shop.

Construction: The room measures 4.7m by 4.7m overall and 2.1m across each gable end. The hinged door is replaced with a folding concertina-type door. Construction begins at Levels 1 and 2, most of which is on shelves bracketed to the walls. There are floor supports for the Brockholes baseboard and the crawl-under bridges. The latter allow access from the entrance area to the control area (top) and

to the sitting area (left). The long Holmfirth baseboard is then added at Level 3, incorporating the integral control panel. There is scope for much fine scenic work, particularly at the corners and on the walls, enhanced by rows of spotlights from the ceiling. The greatest chore is to carry everything up three flights of stairs to the attic. Once there, however, the model railway club atmosphere is perfect!

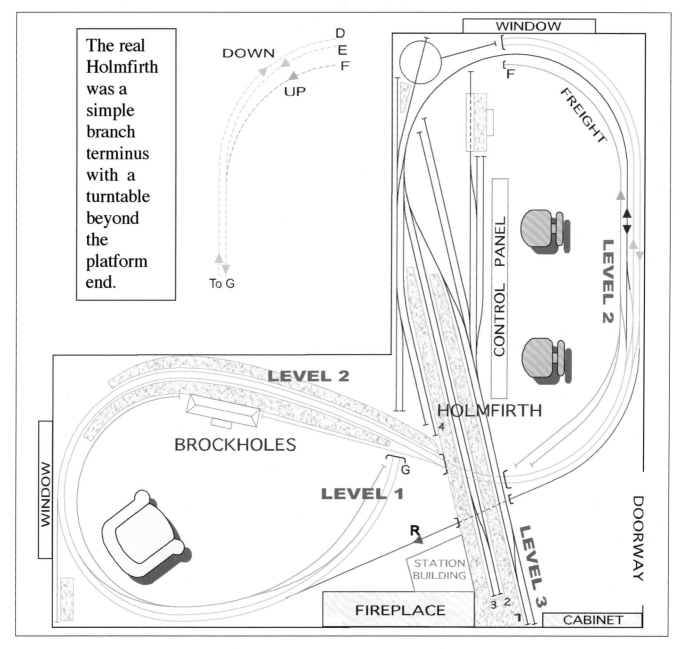

The real Holmfirth was a simple branch terminus with a turntable beyond the platform end.

26

The Huddersfield Loop Mark II

Summary description: An OO gauge out-and-back layout in the attic of a converted cottage industry building.

First inspiration: I had intended to offer here a dockland extension of Layout No. 25 - across the landing and into a second attic bedroom (a mirror image of the first). Inspired by the *North Midland Railway* (Ref.10), it was a single-track out-and-back branch on two levels with a passing station, a docks halt, a lifting bridge and a multitude of quayside sidings. Although too simple to warrant two whole pages, it is reproduced here in simplified form (below), just for interest. In conjunction with Layout No. 25, it would operate as a huge dumb bell with some terminations at Holmfirth.

Second inspiration: Having located Layout No. 25 in *Summer Wine* country and having had an invitation to visit the *Gainsborough Model Railway* (see photos on pages 63, 80 and 81), Marion and I took a short holiday in Holmfirth. A steel spiral staircase led to the attic bedroom and bathroom of our studio flat. This top floor looked ideal for an OO gauge model railway, so I mentally removed all the furniture and ablutions, leaving just the bathroom sink (for tea and coffee). Then I lay back in the bath and designed a second layout set in the beautiful hilly countryside south of Huddersfield.

Design features:
- On the lowest level, a double-track main line oval with two through-stations, each with a goods yard.
- A single-track branch leading to a high-level terminus with a goods yard, MPD and turntable.
- A single-track return loop on the middle level.
- Five levels of construction, with a few short tunnels and all points readily accessible.

Control and operation: Using cab control, four operators are needed for full operation of all lines and yards:
- Main lines (red and blue) - controlled remotely from a master switching panel on the landing.
- Holmbridge station – controlled locally with manual operation of points and uncouplers.
- Diggle goods – controlled locally with manual operation of points and uncouplers.
- Marsden goods – controlled locally, also looking after the reversing loop **R** and Holmbridge MPD.

There are three types of traffic: main passenger, goods and push-pull (Holmbridge to the bay at Diggle). Note the point configurations at Marsden which require trains from Holmbridge to do a complete circuit of the main line before they can take the reversing loop. Similarly, reversed trains must do another complete circuit before they can return to Holmbridge.

When only two operators are available, shunting is suspended

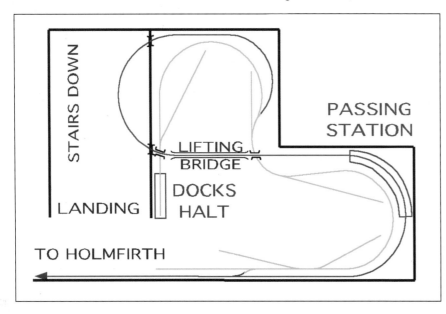

STAIRS DOWN

LIFTING BRIDGE

DOCKS HALT

LANDING

PASSING STATION

TO HOLMFIRTH

at Diggle and Marsden and their goods loops are used simply to hold whole trains. Together with the platform loops at Marsden, three trains can then be in service on each main line (red and blue) - one goods and two passenger - taking turns for a circuit and periodically running up to Holmbridge. In this intensive mode, the main line operator looks after the reversing loop and the Holmbridge operator must pay occasional visits to the bathroom for locomotive turning.

Construction and accessories: The attic is already modernised with thermal insulation, room partitions, good windows and power and light supplies. It is gabled on purlins, with low headroom towards the short wall boards at the sides. To avoid excessive kneeling, some of the baseboards can be built off-stage as separate modules. All baseboards are post-supported from the floor. The room partitions (hatched on the plan) are retained as visual breaks. The attic measures 9.3m by 4.7m overall, with an angled wall at the top end. The gap around the spiral staircase provides an excellent path for the lines between the two through-stations. There is just one duck-under - for occasional access to the trackwork and scenery to the left of Holmbridge. Construction is bottom-up, starting with the main line, then the reversing loop and finally the terminus. On the layout plan (right), railway bridges require a minimum difference of two levels (for example L5 – L3). Although a group of three could have the main line tracks up and running within a couple of years, the total construction time, including buildings and scenery, is likely to be some five to seven years. There is scope for some fine scenic backdrops and much detailing of the platforms, goods yards and

forecourts. Station buildings are all different, being located respectively above, below and level with the tracks, with subway access to the platforms at Marsden. A canal basin could be added.

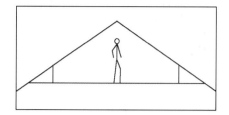

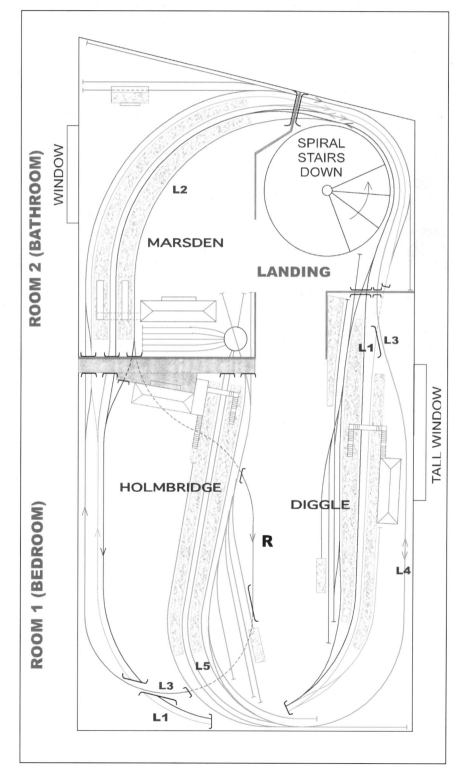

27

The Fustera Garden Line

Summary description: A dumb bell live steam railway and an end-to-end electric rack railway, built in narrow gauge around a Spanish villa in an exotic setting.

Inspiration: During visits to my sister and her family on the Costa Blanca, I relaxed on their sun-lounger and designed a narrow gauge model railway around the boundary. With a height difference of some 1.5m from the front to the rear of the garden, a modestly graded single-track line could be laid around three sides, but the steeply graded fourth side required a rack railway. Light, narrow gauge trains were an obvious choice. I was inspired by the local metre gauge railway which runs between Alicante and Denia, also by two narrow gauge models in gardens: Peter Denny's *Trepolpen Valley Light Railway* (Ref. 56) and Christopher Lepper's *Dingle* (set in Ireland, Ref. 57). The outline at Fustera could be Continental, British, Irish, American or any other favourite.

Narrow gauge options: The choice of scale may well be influenced by a preferred manufacturer of proprietary ready-to-run locomotives and rolling stock. Two common scales suitable for the Fustera line are:

Name	Gauge mm	Scale mm/ft	Scale Ratio
G	45	14.2	1:22.5
SM32	32	16	1:20

(SM32 = *Sixteen Millimetre, 32*mm gauge)

Design features:
- A long single-track steam railway with a passing station on the 'bell' at either end.
- A modest goods yard at two principal through-stations.
- A locomotive servicing and exchange depot at the top station.
- An overhead-wire electric rack railway with two interchange platforms.
- A tunnel extension of the rack railway to a terminus on a stone seat by the pool.
- Secure storage sidings for locomotives and rolling stock on a high shelf in the garage.
- Locos and rolling stock to be proprietary, mostly ready-to-run.

Control principles:
- FM radio control of the gas- or oil-fired steam locomotives.
- Automatic operation and overhead electric feed for the rack railway.
- Manual operation of a service locomotive with rechargeable-batteries.
- Local manual operation of all points and uncouplers.

Operation: Leisurely operation is envisaged for two or three operators with up to four locomotives in steam. One freight and two passenger trains might operate sequentially on the main line, with tablet exchange at the two stations and periodic exchanges of locomotives at Fustera for fuel and water servicing. The rack EMU runs independently in automatic mode. The battery-powered service locomotive is fitted with brushes for track cleaning.

Construction: This could take up to ten years. The site is developed from terraced farmland. The perimeter wall is topped with ornamental see-through concrete blocks. The railway is laid below the wall on the left-hand and top ends. The railway is laid on top of the wall on the right-hand and bottom ends, with a precipitous drop of some 3m to the road below. To avoid buckling, provision is made for thermal expansion of the track between zero and 40°C. (For the faint-hearted, safety fences or nets can be added.) The rack section has plastic racks between the running rails, with a pinion mounted on the EMU driving axle(s). A wooden baseboard is bracketed across the front of the garage. The tops of the garage doors are cropped and a hinged flap comes down to seal the entrance to the storage sidings. The Lido extension runs through a short tunnel with removable roof sections for access. Stations are simple and robust with a few waiting passengers. The trains are the main spectacle, chugging slowly around the perimeter wall. See page 98 for a photograph of Malcolm Morgan's delightful garden line.

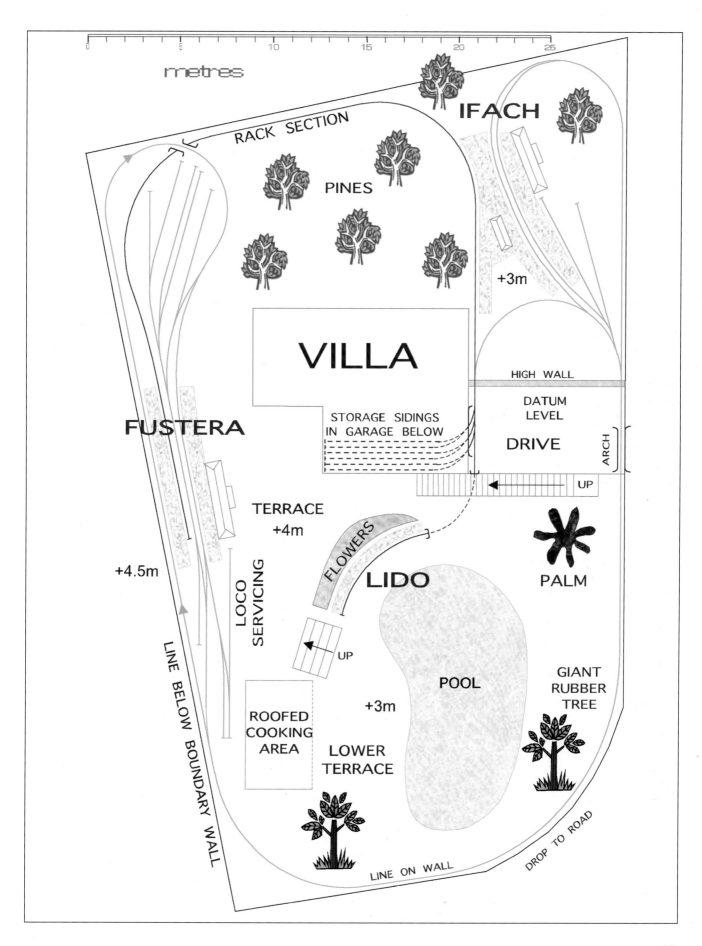

RACK SECTION

IFACH

PINES

+3m

VILLA

HIGH WALL

DATUM
LEVEL

STORAGE SIDINGS
IN GARAGE BELOW

DRIVE

ARCH

FUSTERA

UP

TERRACE
+4m

FLOWERS

LIDO

PALM

LOCO SERVICING

+4.5m

UP

GIANT
RUBBER
TREE

POOL

+3m

ROOFED
COOKING
AREA

LOWER
TERRACE

LINE BELOW BOUNDARY WALL

LINE ON WALL

DROP TO ROAD

metres

Tony Holloway sets up a (Lima) Somerset & Dorset train on his O gauge line at Wimborne. Built some 20 years ago as a simple oval with no points, it is a railway to enhance the garden, not the other way round. It features a tunnel and two showpiece bridges over a pond and waterfall respectively. Tony built this arch bridge himself from aluminium. Many a summer evening is spent enjoying a drink on the patio, right, watching the trains go by.

Malcolm Morgan and his family took eight years to build this scenic SM32 garden line in Gloucester. The radio-controlled, gas-fired locomotive is the Welsh Highland Railway Russell, *made by Roundhouse, with coaches by Brandbright. Malcolm made other locomotives, including 'articulateds', himself.*

A good example of a loft layout between longitudinal purlins is 'Joysford', built by Ken Ross of the Cheltenham Great Western Modellers Group. Named after his wife, the station layout is taken from Stratford-upon-Avon. Track is Peco OO gauge Grade 100 and buildings are a mix of scratch- and kit-built. A Dexion frame supports the chipboard baseboards but the loft is uninsulated, causing some constraints on use. It took three years to build. It was extended into a simple oval with a second GWR station, through scenery of much charm and taste.

Brockholes is featured in Layout No. 25 as a double-track through-station with a bay and a simple goods yard. The real Brockholes of 2002 is a single-track unmanned halt with no bay or yard and with the station building sold off as a private residence. Its gritty, Lancashire & Yorkshire style resembles a Tudor cottage. Some eight decades after the Grouping, several windows still carry a LYR engraving. It is a fine prototype for the model railway.

28

Chicago & Western Loft System

Summary description: A convoluted dumb bell in American coarse-scale N gauge, set in the 1950s with a mix of steam and diesel locomotion. It is a development of Layout No. 14, *The Putnam Division*, but fully occupying my Gloucestershire loft. The aim is to achieve a spectacle of long trains appearing and disappearing over long distances.

Inspiration: W. S. Norris's *Stroudley & Francisthwaite* (Ref. 42) for the great convoluted dumb bell; and John Allen's *Gorre &* *Daphetid* (Ref. 22) for multiple level development in an American setting.

Design features:
- For continuous running - a double-track main line with five through-stations.
- For resting trains and locos at the principal station - six through-tracks and an MPD.
- For interest of movement, shape and colour - two freight depots and marshalling yards.
- For further variety - DMUs or EMUs operate end to end

between terminal platforms.
- For visual intrigue - one split-level station with a connecting stairway.
- For spectacle - a tall curved viaduct across the approach tracks to the principal station.

Geographical setting: Chicago and lines to the west. This allows a wide variety of railroad companies with long trains. Their journeys across the Rocky Mountains to the Pacific Coast were over 2,000 miles long, lasting for days.

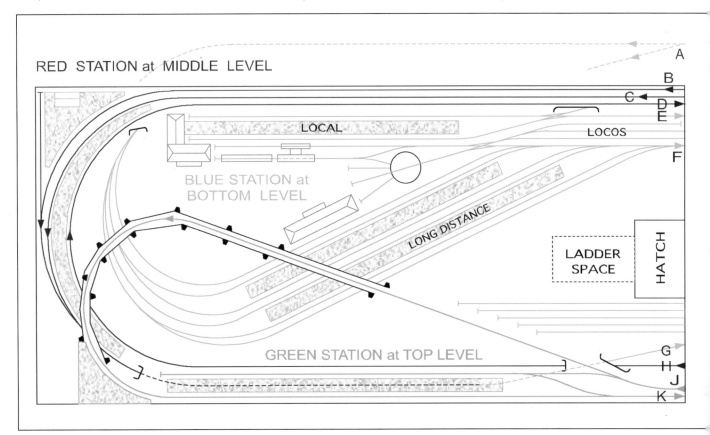

Control and operation: For continuous running of up to six trains on the main line, digital control is ideal. Alternatively, an eye-level cab-switching panel can be used (Ref. 5). With timetable operation, the Traffic Master perches on a stool by the hatch, while local drivers sit at either end of the loft for local movements and shunting. Automatic signalling is triggered by approaching trains and point positions.

Construction: Conversion of my loft is already described in Layout No. 14. This is a now full takeover, using narrow baseboards supported from the floorboards on wooden posts. It is a huge area to fill in N gauge, measuring 12.7m by 3.3m and taking at least five years to build. There is scope for much scenic work, including the four corners - which have removable tops for maintenance access.

A selection of my ready-to-run locos and rolling stock, made in the USA, Europe and Japan by Rivarossi, Atlas, Arnold, Rapido, Alm and Kato. For the Chicago & Western line, I would add a couple of articulated locomotives to head the longest freight trains. (Howard Warren).

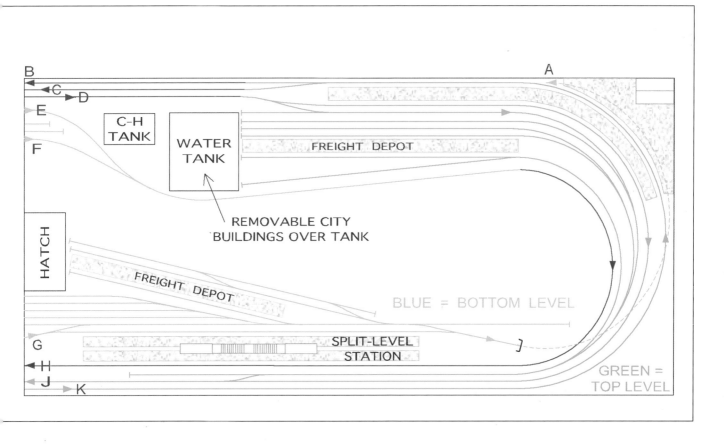

101

29

The Atlantic Coast Garden Railway

Summary description: A complex multi-level O gauge dumb bell with branches and loops, set in a large L-shape garden in my village.

Inspirations:
- The unique L-shape geometry of the site.
- For the quayside, two models: *Port St Lawrence* (Ref. 58); and *Worcester (Diglis)* (Ref. 59).
- For the long, tall, curved viaduct: *Kirtley* (Ref. 33); *Larpool Viaduct* (Ref. 60); *North Devonshire Railway* (Ref. 61); *A Cumbrian Railway in Dorset* (Ref.62); and *Resurgam* (Ref. 63).

Geographical setting: Exeter Central to the Atlantic Coast - the 'Withered Arm' of the LSWR. In a deviation from true history, a new line is built from Halwill to Lydford. This becomes joint GWR/LSWR, as does Meldon quarry (producing granite for track ballast). Served by rival branches from Okehampton, Meldon evolves as an industrial town with seasonal Dartmoor holiday traffic. Its two branch lines have a short connection to make a freight loop.

Control principles: Cab selection and control of key main line points is from a switching panel above Halwill. Main line operators stand in and around Ilfracombe Bay. Local operators control the yards and branches using manual operation of points and couplings. With due regard to safety, wandering-lead

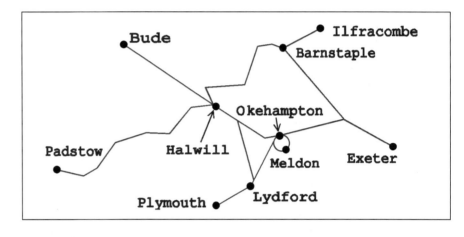

controllers plug into local weatherproof supply pedestals. Any signals are non-operating.

Design features:
- A double-track main line (red on the scale plan) with end dumb bells and branch lines.
- A spectacular front garden features a blue-green painted drive (simulating the River Exe), two ships, two concrete viaducts and two stations integral with the stone wall.
- Five termini and four junction stations.
- A new stone shed has a large window and two doors. It incorporates Halwill at waist-level with storage sidings below at knee-level (**B**) and ankle-level (**A**).
- There is full landscaping with lawns, rockeries, alpines, a few shrubs and some small trees.
- With the ships removed, there is normal access to the bungalow on foot and by car.
- A private garden is retained at the back-left for family use.

Construction: The site is near-level, measuring 72m by 47m overall. The principal civil works are: the new railway shed; buried cables to the control pedestals; two concrete viaducts cast in situ; rockeries and planting out; and a rebuild of the drive to simulate the River Exe. A club of some 15 dedicated members could take a decade or more to complete a project of this magnitude. Maintenance is continuous.

Station track plans (overleaf): Ilfracombe closely resembles its prototype. The other stations have been adapted somewhat.

Operation: In full summer timetable, one Traffic Master and nine satellite operators can run any or all the following services from the 1950s:
- Long passenger expresses take turns of duty on the main line from storage sidings A.
- Like its prototype, the 'Atlantic

Coast Express' splits at Exeter, Barnstaple and Halwill with sections for Meldon, Bude, Plymouth and Ilfracombe.

- Also prototypical, the 'Devon Belle' splits at Exeter with sections terminating at Plymouth and Ilfracombe.
- Local LSWR services run between Ilfracombe and Meldon via Exeter.
- A GWR diesel car serves the GWR branch to Meldon.
- GWR push-pull trains run between Barnstaple and Plymouth via Halwill.
- LSWR push-pull trains run between: Okehampton and Meldon, Halwill and Bude, and Exeter and Plymouth.
- Mineral trains run between Meldon and Bude quay, reversing at Halwill or Plymouth. (The relatively simple track plans of Meldon and Bude are not drawn here.)
- By using the LSWR-GWR freight spur, no locomotive turning is needed at Meldon.
- Pick-up goods trains call daily at all stations.
- Fitted freight trains out of Exeter quay take turns on the main line – one of vans and another of oil tankers.

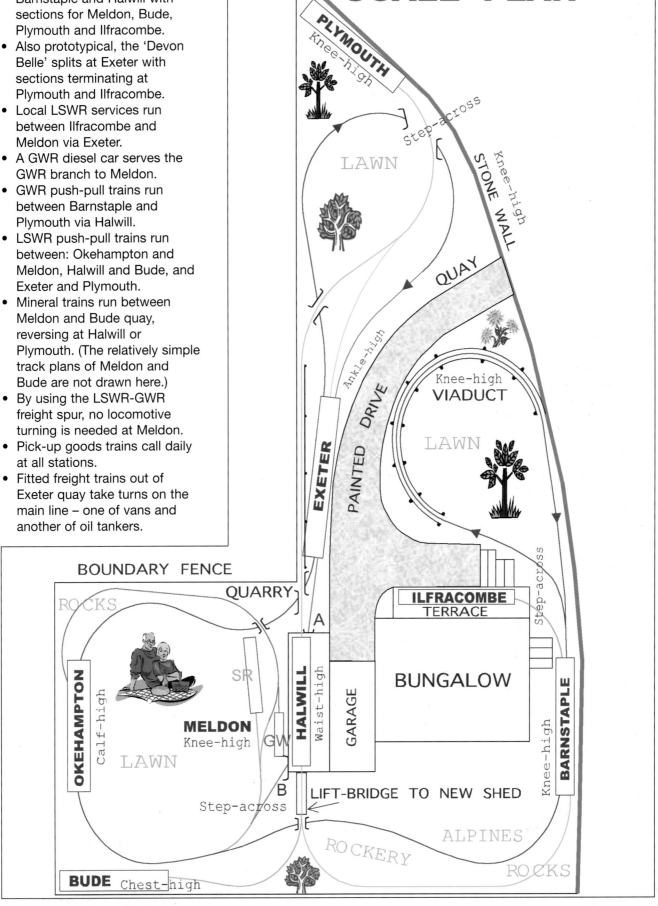

SCALE PLAN

PLYMOUTH
Knee-high

Step-across

STONE WALL
Knee-high

LAWN

QUAY

Ankle-high

Knee-high
VIADUCT

LAWN

PAINTED DRIVE

EXETER

Step-across

BOUNDARY FENCE

QUARRY

ROCKS

A

ILFRACOMBE
TERRACE

SR

GW

HALWILL
Waist-high

GARAGE

BUNGALOW

BARNSTAPLE
Knee-high

OKEHAMPTON
Calf-high

MELDON
Knee-high

LAWN

B

Step-across

LIFT-BRIDGE TO NEW SHED

ALPINES

ROCKERY

ROCKS

BUDE Chest-high

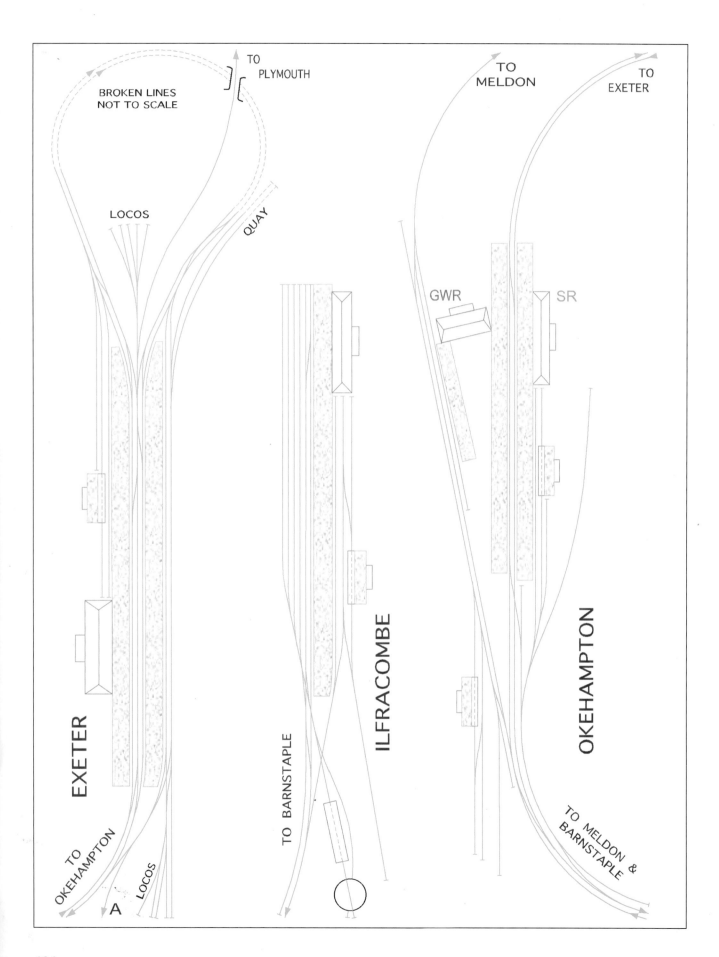

TO PLYMOUTH

BROKEN LINES
NOT TO SCALE

LOCOS

QUAY

TO MELDON

TO EXETER

GWR

SR

EXETER

ILFRACOMBE

OKEHAMPTON

TO OKEHAMPTON

LOCOS

A

TO BARNSTAPLE

TO MELDON & BARNSTAPLE

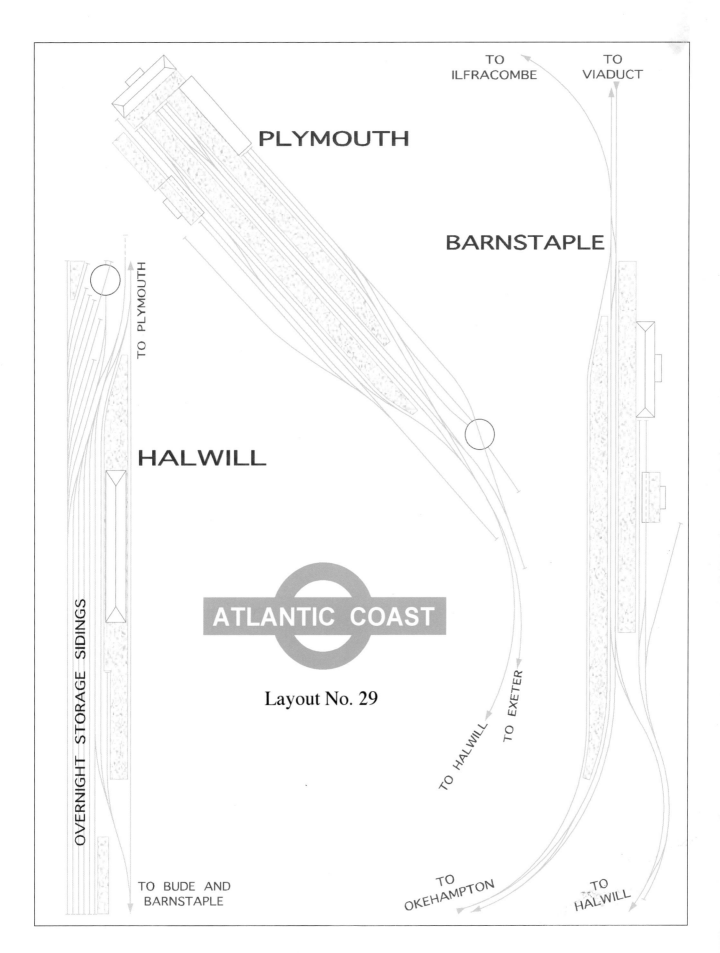

PLYMOUTH

BARNSTAPLE

HALWILL

TO ILFRACOMBE

TO VIADUCT

TO PLYMOUTH

ATLANTIC COAST

Layout No. 29

OVERNIGHT STORAGE SIDINGS

TO HALWILL

TO EXETER

TO BUDE AND BARNSTAPLE

TO OKEHAMPTON

TO HALWILL

30

Gauge One Ultimate Steam Railway

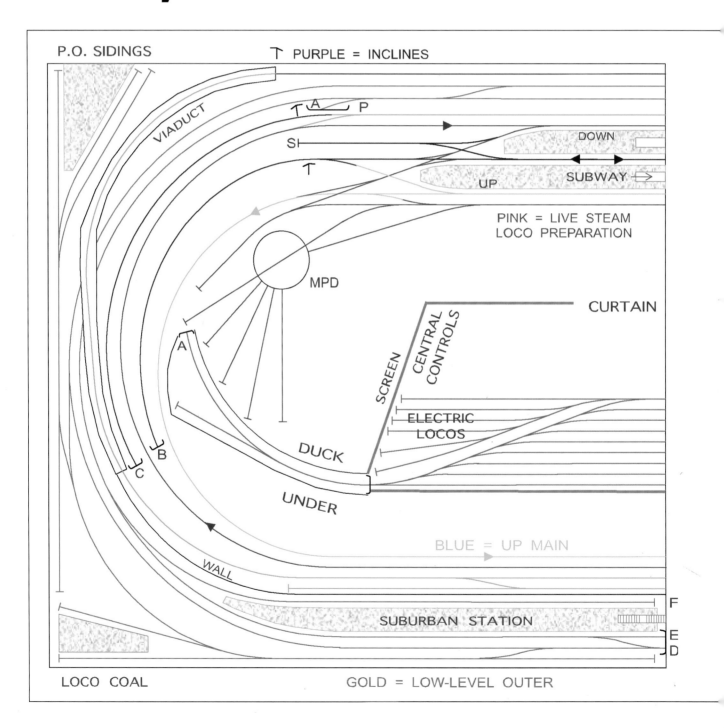

P.O. SIDINGS   ⊤ PURPLE = INCLINES

VIADUCT

A   P

SI

DOWN

UP   SUBWAY

PINK = LIVE STEAM
LOCO PREPARATION

MPD

CURTAIN

CENTRAL
CONTROLS

SCREEN

A

ELECTRIC
LOCOS

B

C

DUCK

UNDER

BLUE = UP MAIN

WALL

F

SUBURBAN STATION

E
D

LOCO COAL   GOLD = LOW-LEVEL OUTER

Summary description: A double-track simple oval at high-level, suitable for live steam in Gauge One. Central storage sidings at low-level. Electric operation around the outside.

Inspiration: For many years, the Model Railway Club undertook the International Model Railway Exhibition (IMREX) at the Royal Horticultural Halls, Westminster.

One of its regular star attractions was the Gauge One Association layout. As well as brilliant live steam performances, peripheral electric-powered locomotives and the occasional EMU, could send a tingle down one's spine. During the 1980s, the main oval for live steam became double-track, supported by a maze of secondary lines, tunnels and sidings at the lower level. This set

my mind racing – what might be the ultimate Gauge One exhibition layout? This plan is a tribute to both the MRC and the Gauge One Association for all the pleasure that they have given us.

Design concepts: Some traditional Gauge One Association principles are applied as follows: 90 per cent all-round access to the inner oval; live steam

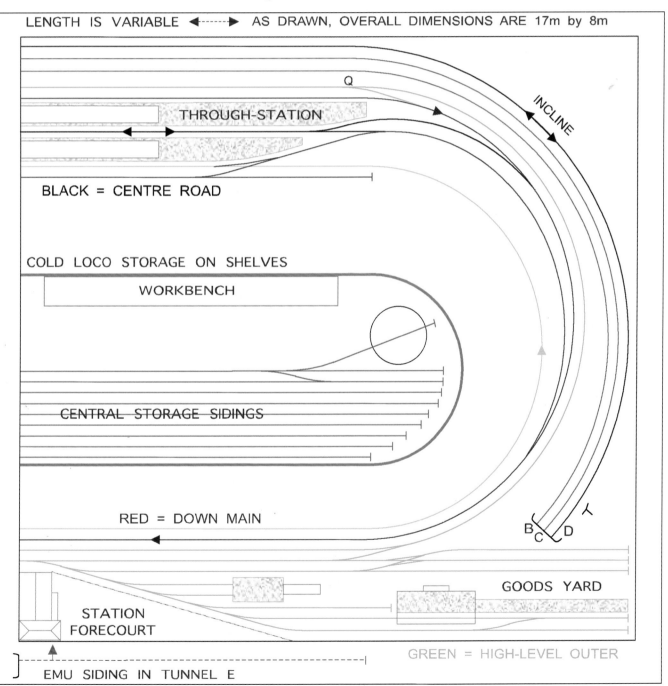

LENGTH IS VARIABLE ◄-----► AS DRAWN, OVERALL DIMENSIONS ARE 17m by 8m

Q

INCLINE

THROUGH-STATION

BLACK = CENTRE ROAD

COLD LOCO STORAGE ON SHELVES

WORKBENCH

CENTRAL STORAGE SIDINGS

RED = DOWN MAIN

B C D

GOODS YARD

STATION FORECOURT

GREEN = HIGH-LEVEL OUTER

EMU SIDING IN TUNNEL E

preparation sidings within the oval; live steam pointwork to be kept to a minimum, especially facing points; a screened central compartment containing storage sidings, a workbench and the central control panel.

My own humble idea is for an incline between the live steam ovals, to permit stock transfers without level crossing of the main lines. At the through-station, the double-faced centre road serves also as the terminal for local passenger trains. Secondly, I have increased the freight activity with a large, discrete goods yard at the upper level and a modest Post Office depot at the lower level. Finally, the outer lines are extended to become a continuous (triple) oval with two passing loops.

Control principles: Electrical control of the various ovals is from the central control panel. There are four local controllers as follows: Central Storage, Through-station, Goods Yard; and PO Yard. The last two are external to the oval, allowing the operators to chat to spectators.

Operation: For full exhibition purposes, the up and down main lines (red and blue) are used exclusively for live steam, with green crossovers **P** and **Q** locked in the straight position. Passenger stock transferring from Central Storage can arrive in any of the three roads at the through-station, with the electric loco reversing or running round into siding **S**. An example of a full steam sequence is as follows:
- Stock arrives in the centre road for a steam loco to back on to the rear for anticlockwise running.
- After stopping in the up platform, a fresh loco on the rear steams the train on to the down main.
- After some clockwise running,

the train stops in the down platform for an electric loco from siding **S** to back on to the rear for return to Central Storage.
- Live steam locos return via pink to the MPD for cooling off or for fuel and water re-filling.

The above sequence may take some 30 minutes to complete. At the same time, electric-powered trains provide interest on the green-gold triple oval, including freight (usually clockwise), parcels (usually anticlockwise), and the occasional passenger train (in either direction). Local passenger trains run as follows:
- A London Transport tube train of 1938 stock (which can be stored in tunnel **E**).
- A Southern Railway 4-SUB multiple unit (which generally

terminates at bay **F**).
- A short steam passenger set (using a second loco from siding **S** at the through-station).

If live steam is restricted to the up main line, green crossover points **P** and **Q** can be unlocked, allowing goods, parcels, local passenger and special trains to run on the down main.

Construction: Baseboards are built in a modest room, using two at a time. At exhibitions, a small army of group members lays the baseboards on a Dexion support frame. Electrical connections and final scenery are then added in situ. The former IMREX layout took some 30 man-days to erect, making this 'ultimate' layout probably too formidable.

Some of the Gauge One Association layouts are owned by regional groups, others are privately owned. One of the latter is Midsomer Norton, seen here in 2001 at the NEC exhibition on its inaugural outing. The layout comprises a double-track oval with the rural through-station on one side, a long viaduct along the other, and a loco preparation MPD in one corner. Two smartly attired owners, Mike Barrett (right) and his son Anthony (left), attend to track-cleaning and steam-raising while a long LMS train passes by. Note the tea mug, oilcan and electric fan on the right-hand loco for steam raising.

References

The references which follow give source lists of magazines, books and videos. The source lists are not necessarily exhaustive. See page 110 for a glossary of magazine abbreviations.

1.   C. J. Freezer, *The Model Railway Design Manual* (Patrick Stephens, 1994).

2.   Norman Simmons, *Railway Modelling* (Patrick Stephens, 1993).

3.   Roger Amos, *Complete Book of Model Railway Electronics* (Patrick Stephens, 1998).

4.   S. J. Dickson, *'O' Gauge in a Small Space* (MRN March 1960). End-to-end, outside 3-rail O gauge.

5.   Tony Walker, *Control Panel Airline Style* (RM December 1993). Reversing loop, 2-rail HO gauge.

6.   John Langan, *Presson* (MRN June 1962). End-to-end, 2-rail EM gauge.

7.   David Jenkinson, *The Kendal Branch* (RM November 1985, July 1988). Dumb bell, 2-rail O gauge.

8.   Ken Payne, *A New Beginning* (RM August 1981). Dumb bell, 2-rail O gauge.

9.   P. D. Hancock, *The Craig & Mertonford Light Railway* (RM November 1955, February 1956, December 1967, June 1978, December 1979 and April 1980). Simple oval, 2-rail OO plus a narrow gauge system and trams.

10. Jeff Colledge, *The North Midland Railway* (MRC Annual 1979 and 1981). Complex out-and-back, centre 3-rail OO gauge.

11. Iain Rice, *The East Suffolk Light* (MR, May 1984). End-to-end, 2-rail P4.

12. Iain Rice, *Woolverstone* (RM May 1990; MRJ No. 39). End-to-end, 2-rail P4.

13. C. R. Miller, *Layout in the Loft, Practical Advice on Conversion etc* (RM October 1986).

14. The Model Railway Club, *Copenhagen Fields* (RM April 1989; MRJ Nos 43 and 46). Complex ovals, 2-rail N gauge.

15. Weston Railway Modellers, *Grove Park* (RM September 1991). End-to-end, 2-rail and 4-rail EM gauge.

16. Dick Yeo, *Epton* (RM October 1978; PMR February 1988). End-to-end, 2-rail and 4-rail Underground OO gauge.

17. Gauge One Model Railway Association layouts (MRN April 1959 and April 1960; RM May 1971, April 1988, April 1991 and October 2000). Simple ovals, live steam and 2-rail electric, Gauge One.

18. C. A. Parfitt, *Going Underground* (RM April 1983). 2-rail OO gauge under the floorboards.

19. R. D. Hart, *The Modelling Possibilities of London's Underground System* (MRC July 1965).

20. C. L. Fry, *Irish International Railway & Tramway System* (MRC November 1961; RM April, October and November 1949, May and June 1956, May 1971). Complex ovals, centre 3-rail O gauge plus narrow gauge system and trams.

21. Peter Haddock, *Wannetka, Warlock & Western* (RM November 1967 and September 1971). Dumb bell, 2-rail HO gauge.

22. John Allen, *Modelling with John Allen* (Linn H. Westcott, Kalmbach Books, 1982); also *The Gorre & Daphetid Railroad* (RM September 1968). Complex multi-level end-to-end, 2-rail HO gauge.

23. Rev Peter Denny, *Buckingham Great Central* (book by Peco Publications & Publicity, 1972; RM July 1958, June 1961, June 1963, September 1969, February 1971, April, July and September 1972, February and December 1978, August 1987, July 1989; MR May 1979; MRJ No. 46). End-to-end, 2-rail EM gauge.

24. C. J. Freezer, *Plans for Larger Layouts* (booklet by Peco Publications & Publicity, 1960). Also by the same author and publisher: *Plans for Small Railways* (1958) and *Track Plans* (1964).

25. C. J. Freezer, *The Potential of N Gauge* (RM September 1966). Reversing loop, 2-rail N gauge.

26. Keith Ladbury, *GWR and LMS Lines* (MRN September 1965). Multi-level end-to-end, 2-rail OO gauge.

27. Michael Foster, *Hornby Dublo Trains* (New Cavendish, 1980). Simple ovals and reversing loops, 3-rail OO, 2-rail OO and French AcHO gauges.

28. Ron Edwards, *Melford & Tawton* (PMR, November 1987). Simple oval, OO gauge.

29. Daniel R. Gallo and Frederick A. Kramer, *The Putnam Division* (Quadrant Press Inc, 1981).

30. Barrie Walls, *Wallsea Main* (RM January 1977, MRC August 1982, January 1987 and October 1992; YMR December 1985). Simple oval, 2-rail O gauge.

31. Manchester Model Railway Society, *Wheatstone Bridge* (RM December 1965 and December 1983). Simple oval, 2-rail OO plus trams.

32. Keith Robins, *Rhosteigne* (RM October 1992). Simple oval, 2-rail N gauge.

33. Don Neal, *Kirtley* (RM August 1969 and August 1970). End-to-end, 2-rail O gauge.

34. G. E. Bigmore, *Bigston to Archway* (RM July 1955). Out-and-back, stud-contact, O gauge.

35. Ken Payne, *The Tyling Branch* (RM April 1957). End-to-end. 2-rail EM gauge.

36. Leamington & Warwick Model Railway Society, *Walford* (RM March 1988). End-to-end, 2-rail EM gauge.

37. Alan Parker, *Kettlewell* (RM December 1983 and November 1987). End-to-end, 2-rail N gauge.

38. S. W. Stevens-Stratten, *South for Moonshine* (MRC Annual, 1979, MRN June 1958). Out-and-back, 2-rail OO gauge.

39. Harry Fisher, *Cornwall & Devon* (MRN February 1960). Multi-level end-to-end, 2-rail OO gauge.

40. John Jay, *London, Bristol & South Wales* (RM July 1969). Complex out-and-back, 2-rail OO gauge.

41. The BR Brighton Staff Association's layout (RM June 1969). Complex out-and-back, OO gauge.

42. W. S. Norris, *Stroudley & Francisthwaite* (*MRN*, June 1957, February and April 1960, May 1961; *RM* May 1980 and Special Extra 1980). Dumb bell, 2-rail O gauge.

43. *The Maycroft Railway* (*MRN* April 1959 and April 1962, *RM* May 1969). Reversing loop, 2-rail O gauge.

44. Bury St Edmunds Model Railway Club, *Abbotsford* (*RM* May and June 1978). End-to-end, 2-rail OO gauge.

45. J. R. Wall, *Hebdon Junction* (*MRC Annual*, 1981). Simple oval, OO gauge.

46. W. F. Dyer, *Borchester Town Station* (*MRN* December 1959). Simple oval, 2-rail OO gauge.

47. F. Eggleton, *Steam Power in O Gauge* (*MRN* September, October and November 1957).

48. Norman Eagles, *The Sherwood Section of the LMSR* (*RM* October and December 1955, July 1968, February 1969, June 1971; *MRN* August, September and November 1957; *MRC* December 1978). Complex out-and-back, clockwork O gauge.

49. *Bromford & High Peak* (*MRC* March 1979, *RM* December 1979 and January 1980). Complex ovals, 2-rail O gauge.

50. West Lancashire O Gauge Group layout (*MRC* November 1960). Four-track simple oval, 2-rail and stud-contact.

51. J. P. Clifton, *Pacific Seaboard Lines* (*RM* September 1976). Multiple ovals, 2-rail O gauge.

52. David Yule, *Abingdon* (*RM* October 2001). End-to-end, 2-rail O gauge.

53. The Gainsborough Model Railway Society layout (Souvenir brochure; *Mrail* October 2001; *Mrail Video 7*, 2001). End-to-end, 2-rail O gauge.

54. Ian Hamilton, *Christmas Magic* (*RM* January 1986). Simple oval, 3-rail Hornby Dublo.

55. Huddersfield Railway Modellers, *Beammas Junction Rejuvenated* (*RM* September 1990). Figure-of-eight, 2-rail OO gauge.

56. Peter Denny, *Trepolpen Valley Light Railway* (*RM* August 1967 and one chapter of the book, Ref. 23). End-to-end, narrow gauge garden line.

57. Christopher Lepper, *Dingle* (*RM* August 1990). Out-and-back 10mm narrow gauge garden line.

58. Peter Smith, *Port St Lawrence* (*RM* July 1984). End-to-end, 2-rail OO gauge.

59. J. F. Webster, *Worcester (Diglis)* (*RM* March 1991). End-to-end, 2-rail O gauge.

60. Mike Cook, *Larpool Viaduct* (*RM* May 1982). 2-rail O gauge in the garden.

61. Ken Northwood, *North Devonshire Railway* (*MRC* January 1978; *RM* August 1978). Reversing loop, 2-rail OO gauge.

62. D. Ward, *A Cumbrian Railway in Dorset* (*RM* August 1984). Figure-of-eight, 2-rail O gauge.

63. Robin St John Lumley, *Resurgam* (*RM* August 1989). Simple oval, 2-rail 16mm narrow gauge.

Abbreviations

BR	British Railways
DMU	Diesel multiple unit
EMU	Electric multiple unit
EWS	English Welsh & Scottish Railway
HD	Hornby Dublo
LED	Light emitting diode
MPD	Motive power depot
MRC	Model Railway Club
NEC	National Exhibition Centre
NYC	New York Central System
psi	Pounds per square inch

Magazines (past and present):

BRM	*British Railway Modelling*
MR	*Model Railways*
Mrail	*Model Rail*
MRC	*Model Railway Constructor*
MRJ	*Model Railway Journal*
MRN	*Model Railway News*
PMR	*Practical Model Railways*
RM	*Railway Modeller*
YMR	*Your Model Railway*

Pre-Grouping railways:

GCR	Great Central Railway
GER	Great Eastern Railway
GNR	Great Northern Railway
GWR	Great Western Railway
LBSCR	London, Brighton & South Coast Railway
LDCR	London, Chatham & Dover Railway
LNWR	London & North Western Railway
LSWR	London & South Western Railway
LYR	Lancashire & Yorkshire Railway
Met.	Metropolitan Railway
MR	Midland Railway
NBR	North British Railway
NER	North Eastern Railway
S&D	Somerset & Dorset Joint Railway
SER	South Eastern Railway
SECR	South Eastern & Chatham Railway

Grouped railways ('Big Four'):

GWR	Great Western Railway
LMS	London Midland & Scottish Railway
LNER	London & North Eastern Railway
SR	Southern Railway

Acknowledgements

Pages

All photographs are by the author except those by:
   Hugh Ballantyne who kindly contributed two photographs of BR steam.   16, 62
   Howard Warren of Cirencester Camera Club for three close-up photographs of my models.   39, 65, 101
   Graham Keene and his friend who photographed the author with his Hornby Dublo train set.   112

Peco Publications kindly allowed two items of material to be republished from *Railway Modeller*.   86, 92

The following kindly made model railways available for photographs:
   Paul Jones and Warley Model Railway Club gave access to the NEC 2001 Exhibition.
   Bob Alderman, exhibitor at the NEC 2001 Exhibition.   6
   Wingfield Railway Group, exhibitors at the NEC 2001 Exhibition.   7
   John Webb, exhibitor at the NEC 2001 Exhibition.   8
   Mike Barrett, exhibitor at the NEC 2001 Exhibition.   108
   Phil Dawling gave access to the 2002 Spring Open Day of the Weymouth Model Railway Association.
   Modern Image Group, exhibitors at the Weymouth 2002 Open Day.   63
   Pen Mill Group, exhibitors at the Weymouth 2002 Open Day.   73
   Phil Dawling, exhibitor at the Weymouth 2002 Open Day.   73
   Richard Brown gave access to the 2002 Mendip Model Railway Exhibition.
   Andy Jones, exhibitor at the Mendip 2002 Exhibition.   53
   Don and Gloria Hillyar, exhibitors at the Mendip 2002 Exhibition.   88
   Tony Holloway gave access to his garden railway.   98
   Malcolm Morgan gave access to his garden railway.   98
   Ken Ross gave access to his loft railway.   99
   Mark Higginson gave access to the Derby Industrial Museum model railway.   82
   Don Handley and members of the Gainsborough Model Railway Association.   63, 80, 81

Finally, thanks to my wife, Marion Postlethwaite, who assisted with much of the indoor photography during 2002.

Index

Hornby Dublo has the last word with two pictures from the author's childhood in the early 1950s:

Above: People of all ages can enjoy Hornby Dublo or a modern equivalent tabletop railway. In this view, Alan shows his grandmother an unlikely mixed train of LMS coaches and an oil tank wagon, headed by Stanier Pacific No. 6231 Duchess of Atholl. *The location is the large front room used in Layout No. 18. (Photo by Graham Keene and his friend)*

Left: The author's only venture into garden railways was this ad hoc terminus laid out on an old packing case, propped on the sill of the French windows. The layout was out and back into the lounge but the station had no turning or run-round facility. The pleasure was in building it. Two train sets were combined here, owned respectively by the author and his friend David from Layout No. 5. The wooden signalbox and station were made by a family friend, Andy Andrews, who had recently emigrated with his family to Australia.

Epilogue: The author's Hornby Dublo train set grew over some five years to six manual points, a diamond crossing, two locomotives, three coaches, six wagons and associated track. This modest collection gave enormous pleasure and satisfaction through numerous layout designs. It is common practice to start modelling modestly and to let more complex layouts evolve slowly - first in imagination, then on paper and finally in timber, metal, plastic and card. Standards also improve gradually as an 'eye' is developed, not only for accuracy and authenticity but for those magic final touches which occasionally emerge from the artistic genius that lurks within us all. The best model railways simply tap into this genius to produce layouts which can stir the soul.